The *Greatest* Sales & Market

CW00557289

The Practical Action Guide for a Small Business

Written by Peter Hingston

Illustrations, cartoons and graphic design by Charlotte Hingston

Copyright © 1994 by Peter Hingston. All rights reserved. 3rd Edition.
Previous editions: Copyright © 1989, 1992. Revised/Reprinted: 1990.
Foreign language editions: Polish (1992), Ukrainian (1994).

Published by Hingston Associates,
Westlands House, Tullibardine, by Auchterarder, Perthshire PH3 1NJ. Tel: 0764 662058.

Printed in Great Britain by Hobbs the Printers of Southampton.

ISBN 0 906555 17 5

Introduction

Although this book has been written for a new or recently started business, good sales and marketing are essential skills for any business to survive and prosper, particularly when times are tough.

Too many books on sales and marketing spend a great deal of time covering the theory of the subject, whereas what is really needed by the small business owner is a guide with practical techniques which he or she can apply immediately to their own business. This down-to-earth approach is what I have tried to achieve with this book. You will find it packed full of ideas to increase your sales (even in a recession) with many worked examples.

You will probably have little to no spare time, so please don't feel you have to read the book from cover to cover, just dip into the section which is of immediate interest.

If you have not already made contact with your Local Enterprise Agency, T.E.C. (L.E.C. in Scotland) or business development unit, remember they are there to help you and much of their advice is free. Look under "Enterprise Agencies" in the Yellow Pages.

I hope you find this book both interesting and useful for your own business.
With best wishes for good sales.

Peter Hingston

Acknowledgements

Charlotte Hingston   For all the illustrations and cartoons together with suggestions for the text, proof reading, final paste-up and the encouragement necessary to complete this project.

Jimmy Walker   For detailed analysis, comprehensive suggestions for the text and corrections to the grammar.

I am also indebted to the following who read sections, chapters or complete draft manuscripts and who provided many suggestions which have been incorporated in the final version.

Tim Atterton	Durham University Business School
Alastair Balfour	Insider Publications, Edinburgh
Sandie Barker	Sandie Barker Associates, Public Relations, London
Elizabeth Cameron	Scottish Council Development & Industry
Alan & Liz Cochrane	Kall-Kwik Printing, Glasgow
Edward Cunningham	SDA & Visiting Professor of Business Strategy (Univ. of Stirling)
Jennifer Forbes	SDA (Advertising)
Paul Golden	Marketing Director
David Hingston	Procurator Fiscal, Dingwall
JA Lyall	McNaughtan & Sinclair Printers, Glasgow
Lilian Morris	
Stuart Ramsden	Chartered Accountant, Glasgow
Agnes Samuel	Glasgow Opportunities

In addition I would like to thank the following for their kind assistance.

Consumer and Trading Standards Department, Strathclyde

WGA Flockhart	Alex Lawrie Factors
James Gordon & Jacky Wilson	Radio Clyde
Paul Huxford	Paul Huxford (Fareham)
Nora McBain	McNaughtan & Sinclair Printers, Glasgow
Sarah Walker	
Alan Wallace	Dun & Bradstreet
Simon Walter	Kall-Kwik Printing
Mike Whitaker	

Finally, I must acknowledge the many other small business people who, knowing that I was writing this book, took the time to share their sales and marketing experiences so that others might learn through this book, rather than having to learn the hard way.

(Note: Appointments are as of 1989 when the first edition was written).

Contents

The Need

Many people on starting a business spend a great deal of time thinking about the technical details — what colour to have their shop decor, what type of cash till to use, what design of packaging their new product should have or what their new glossy brochure should look like. Frequently too little time is spent thinking about their likely customers and how the business is going to achieve a sufficient volume of business. The technical details may be important but you should not lose sight of vital issues, such as:

● *Who are my likely customers?*
● *How will I tell them that I exist?*
● *Why will they use my business?*
● *What am I offering that my competitors are not?*

These are all called "marketing" issues and if not given proper thought, the business is unlikely to succeed. But even if this is done properly and potential customers contact you, a sale is not guaranteed. Just read how various actual businesses lost a sale even when a potential customer was willing to make a purchase . . . . .

1. The lost car sale The enthusiast driver of a prestige car received regular (and expensively produced) news-letters direct from the car's manufacturer. This same firm spent a great deal of money advertising their cars in the national press, but no salesperson from the local dealer, who serviced his car, ever picked up a phone or wrote to ask when the driver was next in town to see the new models, or get a free valuation of his existing car as a trade-in.

2. The lost print job A small specialist printer of labels was approached and asked for a quote. The specification of the first label quoted was not what the customer required so he phoned and talked it through and a second revised quote was produced. Nobody from the label company ever followed up the quote and the customer in fact used another label printer who did phone.

3. The lost leisure club member A lady visited a leisure club and was given a tour of the facilities. She was suitably impressed enough to leave her business card. The Club said they needed new members but nobody took the trouble to phone the visitor to encourage her to join.

4. The lost contract A builder was approached to give a quote to do a job. The potential customer took the trouble to visit the contractor then followed up with a letter requesting a quote giving full details of his requirements. Despite several chasing phone calls and assurances that a quote was on its way, the customer never received a quote from the builder.

5. The lost retail sale A shopper visited a specialist shop and requested a specific product. The shop assistant told the shopper that it would take "months" to order the item, without taking the trouble to contact the supplier (in fact the manufacturer could supply the item within a week).

6. The lost travel commission A business woman visited a travel agent to find out the cost to fly to several cities in the United States. The travel agent worked out an itinerary and cost but never followed up to see why the business woman did not take up the offer.

7. The lost trade customer A specialist sub-contractor, who normally did good work, made a complete mess of one particular job. The boss of the firm never apologised to the customer and the firm's attempts to rectify the faults were a comedy of errors. So the customer took his business elsewhere.

8. The lost overseas order A buyer stepped on to a trade stand to enquire about the products on display. He was given the proverbial "push-off" as the young salesman was pre-occupied with something at the time. If the salesman had only listened for a few moments, (and shown a little courtesy) he would have discovered that he was talking to an important overseas buyer.

In conclusion, for a business to survive and prosper, both its marketing and sales must be done properly.

"In our company, Mr Twitnit, you keep all market research...even the bits you think I won't like!"

Sales & Marketing

Define The Objective(s)

Obviously there is no point in spending time, energy and money on Sales & Marketing unless there is a clearly defined objective or objectives.

For instance, a general objective might be: to increase overall sales or to increase sales of a specific product line/service or to attract new customers or to counteract a competitor's moves or to increase your share of the market. It would be better if the objective was more precise, eg "to increase overall sales by ..% within .. months", or "to launch a new product X and achieve sales of £.. within .. months", or perhaps "to open .. new accounts in Wales by (date)."

The objectives should be borne in mind particularly when monitoring the response to your promotional activities. Is whatever you are doing, helping you to achieve the objectives you gave yourself?

Market Segmentation

This is jargon to describe the discipline of considering the total possible market in much smaller segments or parts. A "market segment" is a group of buyers with similar needs. In other words, it makes you think more clearly as to just who are your customers. For instance, if you own a ladies fashion boutique, you might think that the potential market is every woman living within a radius of so many miles. In fact the real market is more likely to be women of a certain age range, income group and living much closer or who need to travel past your shop.

People tend to segment their market quite naturally to some extent, but it is really vital to understand clearly just who constitutes your "typical" customer. You might also need to know where your customers are.

Without this knowledge, your whole Sales & Marketing approach will be too imprecise to be very effective. Your scarce resources of cash, people and time need to be focused on that part of the market where there are the best sales opportunities.

Market segmentation is even more vital when considering the launch of a new project. Here you are trying to locate that niche in the market which has a demand for your product/service big enough to support your venture and not already dominated by competitors.

Marketing Mix

Once you have completed the Market Research, decided what segment of the market you are aiming for, decided the best way to enter the market and at what time....then you will want to continue to ensure you have the right Product/service in the right Place with the right Price and backed up with the right Promotion. These are often referred to as getting the right "marketing mix", and are discussed in the appropriate Chapters of this book.

Marketing & Sales Plan

There would be little point in all of this if we did not end up with some sort of plan to work to and so this is considered in more detail towards the end of the book.

Special Situations

Although you ought to be concerned with Sales & Marketing at all times, due to the pressure of other matters that usually impinge on people running their own businesses, the catalyst which suddenly heightens interest in the subject is often when you are confronted with a Special Situation. This might be poor trading causing cashflow problems, or the actions of a hostile competitor. These are some of the situations discussed in the last Section of the book.

MARKETING CONSULTANCY

There is at present Government assistance for marketing through the Enterprise Initiative. This provides specialist marketing consultancy which is part-funded by the Government. The work is managed by the Chartered Institute of Marketing on behalf of the Department of Trade and Industry (DTI). The objective of the marketing consultancy is to look at every aspect of your business and to produce a comprehensive Marketing Plan. For a free booklet entitled "The Enterprise Initiative", phone the DTI, tel: 0800 500 200■

"Marketing is not just about Advertising!"

MARKET RESEARCH

Chapters

Market Research means *finding out* as much as you can about the market-place in which your business is either operating now or in which you are thinking of operating in the future.

Because Market Research may not appear to be essential to the day-to-day running of a business it often tends to drop to the bottom of the priority table and not get done. However, only several hours spent finding out what your competitors are up to or what your customers think of your existing business could lead to a marked improvement in your sales.

In fact, doing Market Research can be not only financially advantageous but also interesting and intriguing. You can soon develop a craving for information when you realise its value to your decision making (and profits!). Market Research is an essential initial intelligence gathering exercise before you launch a new operation. It should thereafter be carried out continuously to ensure that the operation proceeds smoothly and to plan and is not suddenly foiled by a competitor's surprise counter-attack or some other unexpected change in the market.

To give an indication of how important market research is, it is estimated that currently businesses in the UK spend around quarter of a billion pounds per annum commissioning Market Research. This is in addition to all the in-house research.

Opportunities & Constraints

The constant changes in technology, society's habits, politics and the business environment, offer both opportunities and constraints.

Every recession and every boom creates new situations, some good, some not so good. Superimposed on these are regional differences. It is important to recognise this and in addition to be aware of how easy it is to draw the wrong conclusions. For instance, in those areas of the country where there is high unemployment, you might think there are opportunities to provide leisure activities as people "will have a lot of spare time" but of course although they have more time they have distinctly less disposable income!

There are also significant changes happening to the age structure of the population which will create opportunities and constraints. For instance, the proportion of 15-24 year olds, which is currently over 16% of the UK population, is predicted to drop to under 12% by the year 2000.

Businesses, especially those that are the survivors, need to recognise change and adapt accordingly to meet new situations as they occur. Market Research is the means of monitoring those changes. Small companies can use their inbuilt advantage of agility to get one step ahead of their larger rivals.

Market or Product Led?

An important aspect to consider is the difference between a market-led business and a product-led business. Historically, too many businesses were product orientated. That is to say they focused their attention on their products and expected their customers to buy what the company could supply. Common examples of this attitude are the manufacturer who sits waiting for the phone to ring with an order, the shop keeper who stands waiting for customers, the country hotelier who looks outside waiting for a car to stop.

On the other hand, a market-led company creates a more successful situation by producing what the customer wants or needs. Such a company tends to spend more time thinking about its *market* rather than its *products* or *service*. Finding out what the market requires is, of course, an important part of Market Research.

Going Through The Motions

Some individuals, organisations and companies simply go through the motions of doing some "market research" because they have been advised they should do some research. In their minds the success of their business project is unchallengeable and their research is done oblivious of any contra-indications that emerge. This is particularly true with people who are inexperienced in running their own business.

An extreme example of such blinkered thinking is where a business actually takes on staff, premises and equipment *before* any Market Research is done!

Obviously, Market Research needs to be done as objectively as possible, however difficult in practice that may be when you are nurturing your own pet project. It is a hard and expensive lesson to have a project go sour which good Market Research would have probably warned against.

Objectives

Market Research has different objectives depending on whether a new venture or project has to be launched or is already in existence.

For an unlaunched project, the prime objectives are:

> To see if the project is likely to be viable and if so what detail features the market actually wants.

For an existing project, the prime

Market Research — Introduction

objectives are:

> To monitor the performance of the project in the market and to gain as much advance warning as possible of changes in the market so you can respond.

Even if a business is not planning to make any changes, it must at least once a year take stock of the market place it is operating in as there could be important changes which pose either threats or opportunities.

Market Research

Market Research can be thought of in 4 parts:

1. Analysing the Market.
2. Watching the Competition.
3. Test Marketing.
4. Assessing the Project.

The first part, **Analysing the Market,** is to provide an inside picture of the trade, the trends both nationally and locally and an understanding of the needs of potential customers. The second part, **Watching The Competition,** is important not only because the competition can present a very real threat to your venture but also because a great deal of interesting and useful information can be derived from observation of actual or potential competitors. **Test Marketing** is not always necessary but it can be very useful for a new product or service where the other market research is either inconclusive or the scale of investment is such that it warrants further testing. Test marketing is really a matter of "flying a kite" or "putting a toe in the water" to check market reaction with the minimum of investment. This is therefore usually done at an early stage before you are fully committed to the project.

The final part of Market Research is of particular importance for any new venture. The Chapter **Assessing A New Project** brings together all the market intelligence you have gathered in such a way as to hopefully allow you to make sensible decisions based on that information.

These four aspects of Market Research form the following chapters of this Section of the book.

And a final thought on the subject of market research: *"The answer to every question is at the end of a telephone — the only problem is knowing which number to ring"* ■

---

10 Common Errors In Market Research

1. Speaking to everyone except the likely buyers.
2. Ignoring warning signals because you are so convinced the project will work.
3. Asking loaded questions, the answers to which simply confirm your ideas without revealing the real thoughts of the person being questioned.
4. Forgetting that often only 20% of the customers provide 80% of the turnover.
5. Assuming you will compete effectively simply because your prices will be lower.
6. For a new venture, being influenced by your contacts who promise to supply you with lots of work when you start. (Ask yourself how they are getting by without you at the present time).
7. Underestimating how long it takes to enter any new market and secure a reasonable market share (years....not months).
8. Failing to recognise the strength and the potential reaction of the competition.
9. Forecasting sales on the simple assumption that you will take x% of the market.
10. Forgetting that new ideas take time and money to introduce to the market.

Analysing The Market

When you are working in any trade or profession you will automatically accumulate market intelligence while conducting your business. Here we consider simple ways to accelerate that learning process.

Though the acquisition of good intelligence information is important to all business and should be consciously pursued on a regular basis, remember if you are considering the marketing implications of a new project or an expansion of an existing venture then this information becomes more vital.

Market intelligence, broadly speaking, falls into three categories:

1. The National Situation where the information relates to social and economic matters. Even if it refers to a specific trade it tends to be general. For instance, it does not usually distinguish between different brands or companies.

2. Trade Information where the information, while still usually on a national basis, is specific to a given trade sector; it will certainly mention individual company names and/or their brands.

3. Sales Data where you have been trading for at least several months, you begin to accumulate precious market intelligence through your sales.

THE NATIONAL SITUATION

Even a small business with a local customer base has to be aware of the social and economic situation at a national level. This may at first seem surprising, but not when you consider that much of our Press, Radio and TV are national in character presenting lengthy and detailed coverage of economic matters. Thus your potential customers are all exposed to national and even international issues. Furthermore, small businesses must survive in a national arena amongst large national and multi-national corporations who may be suppliers, customers or competitors.

Source 1 — The Media

National events, especially crises, can filter down to small businesses with surprising speed. For instance, simply a mention in the national Press or TV that there may be shortages of some commodity will in itself create a shortage because people will rush out and buy whatever is left on the shelves. Equally a gloomy economic forecast can adversely affect sales of luxury goods, the house building sector and so on. Confidence in a national economy appears to have a marked effect on a great number of purchasing decisions made by both private individuals and organisations. Much of that confidence stems directly from what people read in the newspapers or see on TV.

The media also has a profound effect on purchasing "fashions". Most consumers, not just the trendy ones, are influenced by the media and if the media indicates the "right" people are now shifting to buy X and rather less of Y, then heaven help the suppliers of Y if they do not react! Alternatively, heavy media exposure of one particular product, brand or even a particular activity, (eg eating-out, holidays in the Caribbean, DIY or whatever) can lead to a marked swing towards purchasing those commodities.

In fact businesses need to be constantly aware of social changes which may in time affect the market for their goods and services.

Currency exchange rate fluctuations can also be crucial to many businesses. Who would have thought that exchange rates might seriously affect the turnover of a small craft business located in a remote Scottish glen? But of course they are affected for probably a good proportion of their sales will be to American visitors. If the US$ drops in relation to the Pound, not only do fewer American tourists visit the UK but those that come spend less. Thus a 10% drop in visitors, which may not seem large in itself, may translate into a 20% drop in turnover. A business would have to be in a strong financial position to weather that comfortably. Also, as many have found out, there is nothing to prevent such a drop happening two or more years in a row. Such a business should keep a graph of the relevant exchange rates which may help to predict future sales levels.

Long Term Trends The business pages of the quality national and regional newspapers, general business magazines and the various radio and TV business affairs programmes can all give some indication as to long term trends (though surprisingly, there was little warning of either the Oil Crisis of 1973, or the dramatic drop in world share prices in October 1987). Something which the media does give plenty of warning about is legislation which is in the pipeline and can have a direct bearing on a business, eg changes in VAT, changes in commercial rates, bank base interest rates, employment legislation, taxation and so on.

Recognising the trends is important. People who get onto the band-wagon of a new product or service early often do much better than those who come along later, but on the other hand, the

Analysing The Market

early entrepreneurs are exposed to greater risk.

Being slow to diversify when your market is declining can also be a risk. A good example was in the '60s and '70s the media gave much attention to the problems of corrosion on motor cars. A whole industry sprang up providing special after-sale underbody coatings. But with car makers increasing the rust protection on their new cars this large market declined rapidly in the '80s.

In conclusion, the media is an important source of market research information. But since your free time will doubtless be short, you need to be very selective in what you read and what TV programmes you watch for this data.

Source 2 – Government Statistics

The largest concentration of national statistics is gathered by the Government. The cost of compiling all this research is huge and is beyond a small business, but much of that information is available free or at a modest charge to anyone requesting it.

This information can be a revelation to someone who has not seen it before. Comparing one year's figures with a previous year's can indicate trends.

Although much of the information is confined to tables and figures, there are also publications which complement the data with informed comment and illustrated articles. Where there are regional differences, the data may reflect this.

Each government department prepares and publishes its own statistics. However, to help you find the right information and quickly, the government Central Statistical Office produces each year a free booklet entitled "Government Statistics – A Brief Guide To Sources". To obtain a copy, they suggest you phone: 071-270 6364 during normal office hours.

The booklet is a superb source of where to get the statistical data, first listing many publications and then giving the contact telephone numbers in each of the Government Ministries to use if the information you require does not appear to be available elsewhere.

Whereas background reading (as mentioned in **Source 1 – The Media** above) may be an everyday activity, it is sensible to look for statistical data either when considering the launch of a new project or at the annual review of your business.

TRADE INFORMATION

Most industries or trade sectors are fully described in detailed market research reports carried out by specialist commercial research organisations, trade associations and large corporations. With the exception of the last category, these reports are readily available, either free or for a charge.

You could spend all your time simply finding and reading this information rather than getting on with your business, in which case you are likely to become a very well informed bankrupt! To help you avoid this, there are five particular sources that are noted here because they have already done much of the legwork for you.

Source 1 – Trade Associations

First, where a trade has an Association, this is often a great source of information. If you do not already know the relevant Association, it may be listed in the "Directory of British Associations" to be found in any main Public Library.

Source 2 – Market Research Firms

Second, there are a number of specialist commercial market research firms such as Key Note, Mintel, MSI and the ICC Information Group. A selection of Key Note and Mintel reports are shown opposite. Key Note, Mintel and MSI reports tend to have a good deal of commentary as well as statistical data and look at a trade sector overall. The ICC Business Ratio Reports, as their name suggests, tend to concentrate more on analysing the trading performance of a selection of companies in a particular trading sector. These reports can be purchased direct or seen at most major reference Libraries. The addresses for these organisations are:

Key Note (same address for ICC Business Ratios), Field House, 72 Oldfield Road, Hampton, Middlesex TW12 2HQ, tel: 081-783 0755. Mintel, 18-19 Long Lane, London EC1A 9HE, tel: 071-606 4533. MSI, Viscount House, River Lane, Saltney, Chester CH4 8QY, tel: 0244-681424.

There are, of course, other firms doing market research, but they tend to be more specialised, concentrating on one particular trade sector.

Source 3 – Marketing Pocket Book

A little goldmine of statistical info is available in a small book titled the "Marketing Pocket Book". It is updated regularly and is simply stuffed full with tables of data. Though there is no commentary, the tables themselves are relatively self-explanatory and they provide a fascinating insight into almost every aspect of life in Britain today. Copies can be purchased from:

NTC Publications Ltd, Farm Road, Henley-on-Thames, Oxon RG9 1EJ, tel: 0491-574671. (The 1994 edition costs £14.95 plus £1.25 postage).

Analysing The Market

Source 4 – Trade Publications

The UK is remarkably well served by trade magazines, newspapers and journals ranging through virtually every trade sector and providing authoritative information which should be regarded as essential reading. To see if there is a publication specific to your business, see a copy of the directory BRAD (as described more fully on page 59).

Source 5 – Grapevine

In addition to the more official market research sources, you can usually pick up snippets of information and gossip from suppliers Reps or by chatting to people at Trade Shows. This can be a most valuable source of information.

Caution One word of caution when drawing conclusions from bare statistical data is to consider *how* that data was collected (it may not be accurate) and *when* it was collected (it may now be out-of-date). Even the commentaries may be misleading.

SALES DATA

Once you are trading, analysis of your own sales data is one of the most important and powerful ways to find out what the market is doing and in particular to get feed-back on what you are selling.

To analyse sales requires some record keeping which should be as simple as possible yet provide enough raw information to be usefully analysed.

Every business will have its own priorities in terms of what information is required and these priorities may change fairly frequently. Your record keeping needs to be reviewed so that it is still recording the right sort of information. (Many businesses record information slavishly without questioning why they are still doing so).

Typical broad categories of information you may wish to analyse are:

1. **Sales** What are your weekly or monthly sales figures? More importantly, what are the sales of *each* part or section of your business?

2. **Customers** Who are they? (See Note 1 overpage). What are their preferences? (See Note 2 overpage). Who are your main (ie biggest) buyers and why?

3. **Product/Service** What are your best sellers? Are there variations in sales in relation to time (ie what are the trends)?

MARKET SURVEY REPORTS FROM MINTEL & KEYNOTE
(Note: This is just a small selection)

MINTEL

Advertising	Clothing, Teenage	Jeans
Aerobics	Compact Disc, Players	Jewellers
Air Fresheners/Insecticides	Computers, Home	Kitchens, Fitted
Alarms, Home Protection	Confectionery	Lifestyles, British
Alcoholic Drinks	Cream & Milk	Lifestyles, Women
Anti-Freeze	Credit Cards	Lifestyles, Youth
Aquaria	Crisps & Snacks	Lingerie
Artificial Sweeteners	Curtains	Liqueurs
Audio Visual	Database Marketing	Make-Up
Baby/Pre-School Clothing	Dietary Supplements	Medicines, OTC
Bacon & Sliced Meat	Dining-room Furniture	Men's Outerwear
Bakers	Direct Mail	Men's U/wear & Socks
Biscuits	DIY & Household Retailing	Microwave Ovens
Bread	DIY Handtools	Mineral Water
British Lifestyles	Drinks, Health	Motor Car Insurance
Builders (Housing)	Eating, Healthy	Moving House
Bulbs, Seeds & Plants	Electrical Goods Retailing	Off-Licences
Butchers	Ethnic Foods, Fresh	Pasta
Butter	Female Toiletries/Cosmetics	Perfume
Cameras	Films (Photography)	Pet Food
Car Accessories	Fishmongers	Pharmaceuticals
Car Care Products	Food, Specialist Retailers	Photography
Car Parts	Footwear	Short Holidays (Abroad)
Car Servicing	Fragrances	Skin Care, facial
Carpets	Furniture & Furnishings	Slimming Foods
Cat Food	Furniture, Garden	Sports Footwear
Champagne	Furniture Shops	Swimming
Cheese	Garden Tools	Tonics & Vitamins
Chemicals, Garden	Haircare	Tourism (Holidays)
Chilled Ready Meals	Health Food Shops	Travel Agents
Clothing Retailing	Hi-Fi & Stereo	Wine
	Homes & Housing	Women's Magazines

KEYNOTE

Agriculture:	**Engineering**	Commercial Printing
Agricultural Machinery	**& Heavy Industries:**	Greetings Cards
Battery Farming	Plant Hire	**Retailing:**
Chemicals & Allied Industries:	Scrap Metal Processing	Cash & Carry Outlets
Biotechnology Products	**Finance/Business Services:**	CTNs
Chemical Industry	Direct Marketing	Convenience Stores
Cosmetics	Equipment Leasing	Electrical Goods Retailing
Clothing & Personal Goods:	Estate Agents	Freezer Centres
Baby Products	Franchising	Mail Order
Clothing Manufacturers	**Food:**	Mens Clothing Retailers
Footwear	Confectionery	Specialist Food Retailing
Jewellery	Contract Catering	**Transport/Motor Goods:**
Leathergoods & Accessories	Ethnic Foods	Autoparts
Sports Clothing & Footwear	Fast Food Outlets	Bicycles
Women's Fashions	Health Foods	Motorcycles
Construction	Pet Foods	Road Haulage
& Home Improvements:	Slimming Products	**Travel & Leisure:**
Building Contracting	Snack Foods	Camping & Caravanning
Builders' Merchants	**Household Goods:**	Hotels
DIY	Carpets	Photography
Domestic Heating	China & Earthenware	Records & Tapes
Fitted Kitchens	Cutlery	Restaurants
Housebuilding	Glassware	Sports Equipment
Drinks & Tobacco:	Home Furnishings	Tourism In The UK
Public Houses	**Office Equipment:**	Toys & Games
The Off-Licence Trade	Photocopiers	Travel Agents
Wine	Word Processors	**Other Goods & Services:**
Electrical & Electronics:	**Packaging, Printing,**	Contract Cleaning
Home Computers/Software	**& Publishing:**	Giftware
	Bookselling	Security

Analysing The Market

4. Sales Staff How do their individual performances compare?

Note 1: If your customers are the general public, the answer may need to be further broken down into age ranges/sex/income groups etc.

Note 2: A difficult task is to analyse what people want when you are not as yet offering it. How you can get an idea of this is by the use of questionnaires (see the end of this Chapter).

Analysing this information is best illustrated in some examples below. Please note that though the examples include a small specialist shop, a fast-food outlet, a small manufacturer and a company using Agents, the methods of collecting and analysing the sales data can be applied to virtually every small business.

Provided your record keeping method is suitable such an exercise can be done in as little as an evening. It is not simply an academic exercise and if you do not learn something very useful from a particular analysis, drop it. Then think about what you ought to be analysing. The sort of questions you should be asking yourself are "What do my customers want from me?"; " Am I giving them precisely what they want?"; "What more could I do?" and "What does each aspect of my business earn in relation to its cost in time, labour and investment?"

Example 1 A small shop selling a range of ladies fashions (skirts, blouses, knitwear, hosiery and accessories) wants to analyse two aspects of its trading — what types of products are selling and in what price bands. This information is vital so that the limited purchasing budget is spent as correctly as possible.

The information required to make the analyses could come from 3 sources — (i) a multi-department cash register; (ii) manual recording of sales or (iii) by regular stock takes. The information may then be presented graphically as it is easier to understand and one suggestion is shown here. Note that for a fair comparison, sales are given in relation to the amount of stock held (obviously you cannot compare sales of two product categories if there is lots of stock of one but little of the other!) so regular stock taking would be required.

The column height represents the total stock while the shaded portion represents the sales total for the period concerned (which could be a month, a quarter or a fashion "season"). A practical complication arises in that in most shops stock is arriving on a continual basis and so the actual stock level is always fluctuating. A simplification to overcome this problem would be to take the initial stock value (of each category) then add all the stock that arrived during the period. It would also be illuminating to repeat the exercise every 3 months and compare the different graphs. Note that both the stock and sales should be at retail prices (including any VAT).

Although this latter information looks attractive as a pie-chart, these can take too long to draw (unless you have a PC computer with suitable software).

In this example, accessories followed by hosiery sell particularly well in relation to the proportion of stock held. A final point here is that although the accessories represent the least sales in terms of total value, the margins are normally higher so *profit contribution* should also be considered.

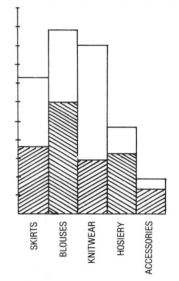

£ STOCK & SALES (At retail prices, inc VAT)

SKIRTS   BLOUSES   KNITWEAR   HOSIERY   ACCESSORIES

BAR GRAPH TO SHOW WHAT PRODUCT LINES ARE SELLING

The same information could be represented another way which would illustrate what proportion of overall sales each category contributes.

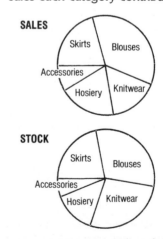

SALES

Skirts   Blouses
Accessories
Hosiery   Knitwear

STOCK

Skirts   Blouses
Accessories
Hosiery   Knitwear

PIE CHARTS OF SALES AND STOCK

The retailer may also wish to examine what price bands are selling best for each type of product — here the sale of skirts is tabulated, for a given period.

The Table clearly shows that the shop should concentrate on skirts up to £40. And since a £20-£25 sale is better than a £10 sale (in terms of overall turnover) the bulk of stock would best be in the higher price range, ie £25-£35.

Example 2 A fast-food outlet offering a variety of food products from a High Street location wants to analyse sales by type over a year. In this example the high rate of transactions excludes the possibility of any manual recording and stock taking data would be difficult to interpret on its own, thus a multi-department cash register would be the typical way of recording sales. This could then be represented graphically as shown right.

Note that unusual occurrences, such as the Chip Frier breaking down, should be noted. This Sales-v-Months graph is a very popular method for analysing sales information. In some cases it may be more relevant to have the vertical column graduated in terms of numbers of customers or numbers of units sold, depending on the business concerned. This information could indicate one product line should be dropped while others could be promoted more at certain times of the year.

Example 3 A small manufacturer (or a company providing a service to other businesses) wants to analyse who their customers are. By looking through past Sales Invoices, the table over the page could be produced. This

PRICE BAND	TOTAL STOCK (of Skirts)	SALES (of Skirts)	SALES (as % of Stock)	SALES (as approx % of Total Skirts VALUE)[1]
Under £10	10	7	70%	3%
£11-£20	21	17	81%	14%
£21-£30	32	24	75%	32%
£31-£40	28	16	57%	30%
£41-£50	15	6	40%	15%
Over £51	8	2	25%	6%
				100%

Note 1: Calculated as follows. For each Price Band, total sales estimated by multiplying the middle of the Price Band by total number of skirts sold in that Price Band, eg for £21-£30 Price Band, multiply £25 x 24 skirts = £600. Doing this for each Price Band gives total sales of approx £1850, so Sales of Price Band £21-£30 represent £600/£1850 x 100 = 32% of overall skirt sales.

£ SALES

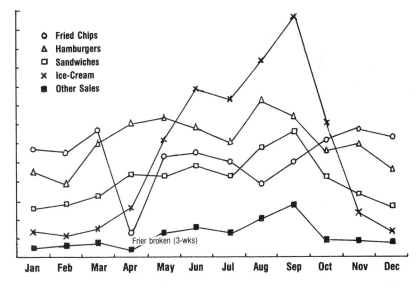

- ○ Fried Chips
- △ Hamburgers
- □ Sandwiches
- ✗ Ice-Cream
- ■ Other Sales

Frier broken (3-wks)

Jan Feb Mar Apr May Jun Jul Aug Sep Oct Nov Dec

GRAPH TO SHOW SEASONAL CHANGES IN SALES OF FAST-FOOD OUTLET

Analysing The Market

information (see right) will indicate which markets are worth pursuing so that your sales efforts are focused on the most promising areas rather than dissipated on less fruitful ones.

Example 4 A business which uses Agents around the country may want to compare sales in each territory. The information would be readily available from the commission payments being made to the Agents and this could then be represented in a graph as shown:

CUSTOMER	SALES PERIOD — (Jan-Dec 1988) SALES (Units) SALES (% of Total)		SALES PERIOD — (Jan-Dec 1989) SALES (Units) SALES (% of Total)	
N.H.S.	510	66%	404	65%
Local Authority	26	3%	33	5%
CEGB	84	11%	75	12%
Export-France	65	8%	85	14%
Export-USA	15	2%	20	3%
Export-Germany	46	6%	0	0%
Others	28	4%	8	1%
Totals	774	100%	625	100% (-24%)

£ Commission (or Invoiced Sales)

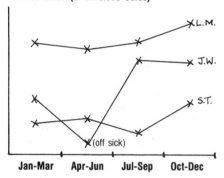

GRAPH COMPARING PERFORMANCE OF DIFFERENT AGENTS

Conclusion Graphical or tabular representation of sales data not only allows you to get a feel for an aspect of the business but it allows it to be discussed easily with a fellow Partner, Director or member of staff. As with any item of market research, however, nothing should be taken in isolation but as a part of an overall picture.

QUESTIONNAIRES

Analysing sales provides excellent historical data but it does not reveal clearly what more you could be doing, nor is it much help in predicting how people will react to a new project.

Talking specifically to both existing and potential customers is the obvious solution to this dilemma. To do that in a proper, structured way it is best done using some form of questionnaire.

Questionnaires pop up in all sorts of places, for instance:

In The Street We have all had the experience of being stopped in the street and asked a number of questions. An adaptation of this is when you are handed a questionnaire to complete while flying or on a train.

Consumer Goods Manufacturers love these! They often suggest that "To register the guarantee..." you have to answer all sorts of personal questions on a questionnaire form. They are frequently too long and ask irrelevant questions, but the concept is good.

Hotel Rooms In this case the questionnaire form is left on the bed or table requesting your co-operation in completing it. The hotel is usually trying to establish how you heard about the hotel (so their marketing campaign can be fine tuned), also if you are on holiday or business and how well the staff have treated you!

In the above examples the questionnaires are all clearly that, but sometimes businesses hide questionnaires in other forms. For instance, when completing a car hire form, or applying for a loan or booking a holiday, spot the extra questions which are not relevant to your particular transaction but are to provide market research data for the company. It can be a very revealing insight into the company concerned as these questions obviously touch upon sensitive policy decision issues within the company.

The point of all these examples is to illustrate how your own business might utilise this very rich source of potential information to the full.

How To Write A Questionnaire
The golden rules of questionnaires are:
* Keep the questionnaire short and simple.
* Do not "load" the questions.
* Do not ask "open" questions.
* Ask only people who are existing customers/potential customers.
* Ask as many people as you can.

Keeping It Short And Simple

Ask yourself, what is it you are trying to find out? Will the answers you get actually help? Ask only the most important questions and avoid any fringe questions. There should be no more than 5 to 10 questions. A multiple choice or Yes/No format is usually best as it is both easier to answer and quicker to analyse.

"Loaded" Questions

Assume you were considering starting a small computer training business which trains staff on word processing and accounts. You might then visit companies locally who you think would have a need to send their staff to you for training to get their views to assess if the business would be viable. Questions such as "Do you use computers for word processing or accounts?" or "How are your computer operators trained at present?" might be reasonable questions but if you were to ask "Would you use us if we offered the best courses?" invites the answer "Yes" as it is a "loaded" question. A loaded question really only invites one answer. For instance in this example the reply is unlikely to be "no"!

It is very easy to fall into the trap of asking "loaded" questions. Try also to avoid emotive or exaggerated phrases in the question. Also, be aware that people often give the reply which they think you want to hear.

"Open" Questions

The purpose of the questionnaire is to find out precise answers to specific questions so you can draw conclusions. The danger of "open" questions such as "Do you think word processing is useful for businesses?" is that it could lead to a long debate! Instead, to each question on the questionnaire the answer should be either yes/no or one answer of a multiple choice. In general, avoid asking for people's opinions — stick to the facts.

An exception to this might arise if you are launching a new product or service and therefore your direct questions may miss some valid point which you have not considered. Giving the person questioned an opportunity to express their opinion or thought might elicit a vital fact. Should this arise in the early questionnaires, a more direct question could then be incorporated into later questionnaires.

Ask The Right People

To reach the right people might involve house-to-house interviews or if doing the survey in the main street stopping only those people whom you think might use your product or service. There may be places that your likely customers congregate. For instance if you were planning to set up a business selling sports equipment obviously you would visit local gymnasiums, athletics clubs etc. Remember when you are interviewing the general public that you do not need the name of the person you are interviewing. In contrast, when interviewing business contacts, it is useful to know who said what as that can provide useful sales leads later.

Ask Many People

Within reason the more people you ask the more accurate will be your survey, provided, of course, that you are asking the right people (ie those who are likely customers). If your likely customer base is very large then you can make your survey more representative by only asking every tenth person you meet or sending out your questionnaire to every tenth name on a list.

To make the analysis of the survey data easier you could type out one questionnaire and photocopy it so that with each person you ask, you complete a new sheet. This makes adding up the figures at the end easier.

For consumers, you need to ask at least 100 people, but for trade buyers you might only be able to ask about 10-20. Business respondents are often interviewed by phone.

How Not To Do It!

This is based on an actual example of a questionnaire produced by a newspaper which was researching the advertising needs of local shopkeepers. Only the first few questions are reproduced here:

Q1   What is your attitude to advertising, and where do you advertise? (Note 1)
Q2   Do you use Classified or Display advertisements? (Note 2)
Q3   What emphasis do you place on displays? (Note 3)
Q4   How do you try to compete with big Department stores? (Note 4)

Note 1.   There are two questions here. Also they have not asked how often the shop advertises.
Note 2.   This is quite a good question but would be better as two Yes/No questions.
Note 3.   Do they mean shop window displays, interior displays or display advertisements?
Note 4.   Although a rather nosey question which people might not answer, it may provide useful information for the newspaper advertising sales people.
General.   The answers to these very open questions would be difficult to analyse.

Analysing The Market

A Good Example

In the example shown right, note the use of simple tick boxes, the gentle request at the beginning and the promotion of related products at the end.

Another good technique is to introduce a little humour. For instance a finance company when asking its trade customers how they rated it, in one question asked "How responsive have we been to handling your general enquiries?" The tick box options were then titled: "First Class", "OK", "Could be better", "Oh Dear!"

And finally, if asking someone to go to the trouble to complete a questionnaire and return it to you then at least provide them with a reply-paid card or envelope or use the Royal Mail's Freepost service ∎

How To Do It Better!

This second example is part of a questionnaire from a computer hardware supplier, enclosed with the product and part of their "user registration".

Would you please answer the following questions which will assist us in our continuing effort to provide you with quality products that meet your precise requirements.

Q1 Where was the product purchased?

Computer Shop ☐   Dept Store ☐   Mail Order ☐   Other ....

Q2 What will be the main use for the product?

Home ☐   Education ☐   College Research ☐   Business ☐

Q3 Why did you choose this product? (Please tick only one option)

Quality ☐   Features ☐   Price ☐   Other........................

Q4 How did you hear about the product?

Saw in shop ☐   Saw advert ☐   Recommended ☐   Other...........................

Would you like to be sent information on the following useful computer products:

Product xxxxx ☐   *Product yyyyy* ☐   *Product zzzzz* ☐

Name ....   *Address* ....

A great deal of useful information can be derived from close observation of your actual and potential competitors.

If your business is already trading, knowledge of your competitors is obviously vital. For instance, are your competitors muscling in on your "territory"? Or are they moving into new markets which you should also explore? Are they changing their product or service, and if so why? Even straightforward price changes can be crucial information. Your competitors may also be planning marketing measures which could jeopardise your own business.

If you are planning a new project and there are companies already operating in the area you plan to enter you can learn from them because in a sense they are doing today what you plan to do tomorrow. As they are ahead of you they will already have refined their product or service, made mistakes, gone up blind alleys and found better ways of doing things. All this is vital intelligence information. Furthermore, as they will be your competitors their strengths and weaknesses merit analysing.

No Competitor? Beware!

Sometimes when a new business idea is dreamed up, the entrepreneur(s) are relieved and excited to find there are no competitors doing what they plan to do. They hope they will therefore be the first in the field and will "do very nicely, thank you".

However, this situation, which is not uncommon presents two major threats. First, the fact that there is nobody doing what you plan to do might mean there is an insufficient market for a business to be viable. In fact, those market areas which are most hotly contested are often those where the potential pickings are richest. Rather like bees swarming around a honey pot! Second, if there is indeed a gap in the market which has potential, it is most unlikely that no-one else has seen it. The reality is that one or more companies might be working on rival plans already. Hopefully the tips below will give an early indication of their activity.

Locating New Competitors

If you are already trading, you will usually be aware of existing competitors though it is most important to keep an eye out for new competition. If you get early information on a potential competitor's plans, it is much easier to make his market entry more difficult, ie slow him down, by considering some of the tactics outlined in the Chapter **Coping With Competitors**. In a surprising number of instances, companies are so blinkered that a new operator starts trading and begins to establish himself before existing companies wake up to his existence!

So how do you get the earliest possible indications of a new competitor who is planning to enter the market? The first point is that you must be aware of this possibility.

One of the best sources of information is trade gossip as the new company will at some stage have to start talking to the same suppliers and customers as yourself. Trade publications can also be good indicators, eg the "Vacancies" columns as the new operation will need to recruit staff at a very early stage, probably prior to trading.

In a retail context, if a shop unit becomes vacant nearby (ie within your customer catchment area) you should make the effort to phone whoever is selling it to establish as much as you can (usually only possible by showing an interest in the vacant unit yourself). In a manufacturing context, close observation of other companies at Trade Exhibitions and reading their advertisements (particularly in the trade press) can both give an early clue to a new competitor's activities.

Locating Likely Competitors To A New Venture

If you are planning a new venture this almost certainly involves operating in a new or enlarged market with different competitors to those you have at present. So how do you track down likely competitors?

If the new project has a localised market:

1. Consult the Yellow Pages and any other local Trade/Business Directories. Between them they will list virtually every business operating locally. You then need to assess each relevant entry (see below).

2. If your intended business is retail, walk the streets in the area where you are thinking of setting up and mark on a street plan the name and location of any competitors. Ask Chartered Surveyors with local knowledge if they know of any business similar to your proposed venture that is also looking for premises.

3. Ask your suppliers' Sales Representatives who else they are supplying in the area. But do note that if they are gossiping about others they are likely to tell others about your plans too!

4. Ask end users who they use at present — this might even show up companies who you would not even

Watching The Competition

have considered as competitors, eg an outdoor clothing retailer might be surprised to learn how many of their well-heeled customers are buying their waxed jackets from market stalls!

If the new project is more regional or national in character, then other strategies are required, in particular:

1. Read not only the relevant trade and specialist consumer press but try phoning and asking to speak to one of the Editorial staff. They are usually very knowledgeable and do not mind talking to someone for a few minutes. Prepare several questions in advance but realise that you will probably be expected to explain who you are and why you are calling.
2. Visit a main Public Library and ask a Librarian if there are any Directories for your proposed business sector. There are so many Directories available these days that, not surprisingly, there are Directories of Directories. An example being "Current British Directories". Well-known Directories include "Kompass" which lists many UK manufacturers by product, giving their address and other information and "Kelly's" which lists over 80,000 businesses in classified and alphabetical sections. It also lists industrial, commercial & professional organisations in the UK. Then there is "Sell's" which lists over 60,000 companies with 10,000 trade names. For the retail sector there is the "Retail Directory" which lists, by name, the buyers and chiefs in most of the main retail groups and some smaller retailers. It also gives a plan view of main shopping streets with the different names of shops annotated. Most of these Directories are updated annually so it is worth ensuring you are reading the most up-to-date edition.

3. Attend the relevant Trade and Consumer Exhibitions. Talk to as many people as possible. Take notes. Here your competitors are at their most vulnerable — their goods are on show and you can usually walk straight onto their stands. However, you should realise that companies operating in any fiercely competitive environment will be taking some defensive measures, eg their Price List may not be out on display and their latest products may either be hidden or only a dummy will be displayed.

Checking-out The Competition

A number of techniques are possible:
1. If a competitor is a limited company, they have to file annual accounts and returns which are available to the public for a small fee. They give names of Directors and financial details. For companies registered in England or Wales these details are available either by visiting: Companies House, 55-71 City Road, London EC1Y 1BB, tel: 071-253 9393 or by post from: Companies House, Crown Way, Maindy, Cardiff CF4 3UZ. Tel: Cardiff (0222) 388588.

For companies registered in Scotland, these details are available by post, by phone or by visiting: Companies House, 100-102 George St, Edinburgh EH2 3DJ. Tel: 031-225 5774.

There are satellite offices in Manchester, Birmingham, Leeds & Glasgow.

For companies registered in Northern Ireland, these details are available from: Companies Registry, IDB House, 64 Chichester Street, Belfast BT1 4JX. Tel: Belfast (0232) 234488.

This data is also instantly available for PC computer users (with a modem) and who subscribe to BT Business Information Services. For more details,

ring Freephone 0800 200 700.
2. If the competitor is a manufacturer or produces any type of product, buy, rent or borrow a sample of their product and check it out noting strengths and weaknesses. Note too any patent markings.
3. If the competitor is in the service sector, use his service or if that is not possible ask friends to phone as if they were potential customers and get them to ask about prices and how soon they can get the service. This may reveal how busy the firms are. This same technique can be used for manufacturers if data on their products is hard to acquire.
4. Obtain pamphlets, sales literature and price lists whenever available, by writing, phoning or at Exhibitions where the competitors have a stand.
5. Photocopy or cut out your competitors' advertisements. These not only give details of the product or service they are offering but may also

"And how many customers have they had today, then?"

give details of prices. More importantly they reveal how competitors are marketing themselves, ie which customers they are trying to attract, the features they are emphasising, the image they are trying to project and any special inducements they are offering, such as low interest finance, quick deliveries, or whatever.

6. Contact local newspapers who might have done an article on the business and if so get a copy. This can be a very revealing source.

7. Speak to their past or existing customers, wherever possible, and take notes.

8. If possible, speak to ex-employees.

Rationalising The Situation

The easiest way to keep track of the market research information you will be gathering is to keep a small file or folder for each competitor. Into these you can put copies of their sales literature, price lists, cuttings, and your own notes which may simply be a scribble from a notepad.

Then, if operating in a particularly competitive field or if you feel under threat from a competitor, you should look through these notes regularly, and take the time necessary to complete an Assessment Checklist similar to the one shown right. You could type up your own Checklist based on this but include only those items of relevance and incorporate other items appropriate to your own situation. Photocopy your Checklist and then complete one per competitor ■

COMPETITOR – ASSESSMENT CHECKLIST

Business Name: ....

Business Address/tel no: ....

Ltd Co, Partnership or Sole Trader? ....

Date Commenced Trading: ....

Other Branches/Subsidiaries: ....

Names of Directors/Proprietors: ....

Other key staff (eg Sales Manager): ....

If Ltd Co, details from annual accounts:

		Directors
Turnover (Year 19.../19...):	£................	Salaries: £................
Profit:	£................	£................
Debts?	£................	£................

Any unusual items: ....

Shareholders/Dividends: ....

Description of business (ie everything they do): ....
....

Details of their products or service: ....
....

Prices (of similar items to yours): ....

Special features (if any): ....

What advertising do they do (which media, how often, what do they stress in their ads?): ....

Other Promotions (eg Exhibitions): ....

Sales Methods (incl incentives, discounts, credit terms, guarantees): ....

Your Assessment of their Strengths & Weaknesses: ....
....

Test Marketing

Test marketing is basically "putting a toe in the water" before fully plunging in. Its function is to test market reaction to a new product or service with the minimum of investment. It is usually done at an early stage before becoming fully committed to a project.

Test marketing is not always necessary but it can be very useful where other market research data carried out is not conclusive or the potential investment in the new project is large enough to require this type of testing.

Its drawbacks are that it may delay the launch of the main production run or service and reveal your hand to any competitors. However its advantages are many. Not only can it quickly indicate the likely level of demand for the product or service, but it also provides feedback to allow fine-tuning of pricing, packaging, design details, overall marketing strategy etc.

Test marketing is not just relevant to a completely new product or service; it may also be relevant to assessing the suitability of a change being contemplated for an existing product or service, such as new packaging, a new pricing structure, a shop re-vamp, new image launch, new market areas and so on. It is therefore not surprising that test marketing activity is a very common practice and can take many different forms:

The Advert   This is the simplest way to check the market though it has limitations. With this form of test marketing a product or service is advertised as if it were actually available (even if it is not quite at that stage) to see what reaction it produces. Of course the normal rules of successful advertising apply (see Chapter **Advertising – How?**). An example of this type of test marketing is where a product is advertised when it is still on the drawing board. A service business which has not yet started is possibly easier to advertise though again some artistic licence may be required. Since you cannot actually deliver the goods or service immediately the wording used must be carefully chosen and must not mislead. Better if the advert encouraged the reader to send or phone for a leaflet or more information.

The Mailshot   In this case you send a letter to any potential customer requesting a response which would indicate their interest in what you have to offer. This can be a very effective technique especially if the customers are businesses and the letters are addressed to named individuals or job titles. It might be a good idea to include a stamped addressed envelope. Even with a targetted business letter, you are likely to get fewer than 10% replying so be prepared to follow up by phone.

The Leaflet Drop   This is a version of the mailshot but less personal and so best suited to the general public by slipping the leaflets through their letter-boxes. It can also be used for trade customers (if sheer numbers are large) where it could be mailed direct like a mailshot or carried loose (called an "insert") in suitable publications. See also the Chapter **Producing A Leaflet/Brochure** .

The Exhibition   Yet another way to judge market reaction to your product or service is to rent a stand at a suitable trade or consumer Exhibition. It is particularly useful because you get immediate feedback from potential customers which can be crucial in fine tuning your product or service. In terms of test marketing, judge the response by firm orders taken either at the Exhibition or immediately afterwards. You may even discover there is little interest in what you are offering!

Scene at a typical Trade Exhibition, which also illustrates "shell" stands as discussed later in the section on Exhibitions.

The Sample If it is a product you are making which is to be sold to the trade you can show samples to potential customers and take orders before committing yourself to full production. This practice is very common in the fashion trade. In some cases it may be possible and useful for a potential user to try out a sample product (at no expense to themselves). This not only allows them to assess the product fully but provides the makers with valuable performance data.

Discussion Groups A good technique used by firms whose customers are the general public, is to invite a group of selected potential buyers to a meeting where they are asked prepared questions and there is some open discussion to assess their reactions to a new product or packaging. Usually some food and refreshments (but no alcohol until the end!) are laid on to make the event attractive (as the participants are not usually paid). The meeting requires careful preparation and handling to prevent getting biased results, eg one bossy person in the group may begin to lead the group's thinking his/her way which is obviously undesirable.

Control Groups A very revealing method of test marketing (which is not possible with all projects) is when you can split your market and try the revised product or service on only part, continuing the former product on the rest as a "control". An example of this was an American consumer magazine that was faced with falling sales and wanted to experiment with a completely new style of front cover design. Instead of having one celebrity on the front cover, they wanted to try a whole montage of celebrities. So for several issues they produced two versions of the same magazine — identical except for their front covers. They then distributed the two in closely defined geographical areas so that sales of the two could be compared. The advantage of the "control group" (ie those readers who received copies of the magazine with front covers similar to their normal style) was that a *comparison* could be made. (It was concluded that those magazines which had the front covers featuring many celebrities sold more).

Trial Area Where you are producing a product which eventually you hope will be sold nationally, a form of test marketing is to first limit the marketing and sales of the product to one area of the country. This is sometimes called a "pilot". Then, if that experiment is successful, the product (perhaps modified in the light of that early experience) can be distributed and promoted nationally. This is often done with foods, confectionery, drinks and toiletry products ■

Assessing A New Project

Many businesses, after they have been trading for a period, consider expanding. This could entail opening a new outlet, launching a new product, entering new markets or perhaps starting a second style of service. These should all be considered as NEW projects.

After you have carried out exhaustive (and probably *exhausting*) Market Research into the new project, you will be faced with trying to make some sense of a huge amount of information, some of which might be contradictory. If you do not carry out an assessment in an objective and disciplined manner there is some danger that your own feelings will intrude and bias the final decisions.

This Chapter looks at 3 ways of assessing any new project. First, we stand back and take a broad look at the project without getting bogged down in the details. Next, we look at the results of the market research in detail, in particular the strength of the competition and finally, we consider the likely impact of the project on your own lifestyle and business.

THE BROAD LOOK

In many cases the ultimate decision to proceed or not with a project rests with the financiers of the project/business. In that case it means that an outsider, a third party, will be looking dispassionately at the project. In contrast, where business owners make the decision themselves, the important safety check of an outsider's view, is lost. So what would financiers look for in a project as likely elements for success? First, they consider the company proposing the project and they ask themselves:

1. **Management** Is there a balance of skills and experience? This covers administration, finance, marketing and sales plus any trade or technical expertise. In a small business this knowledge may be vested in only one or two people.

2. **Finance** Can adequate cash be raised to finance the project including contingencies for unforeseen problems that will undoubtedly arise?

3. **Administration** Are the administrative systems in place, running smoothly, de-bugged and is there a Plan to implement the new project?

4. **Strengths/Weaknesses** What are the strengths and weaknesses of the present business. Does the proposed project make the most of the firm's strengths while taking account of its weaknesses?

5. **Trading Record** Does the past history of the business, however short, indicate it can cope with the changes and stresses that any new project will create?

Next, the financiers look at the project itself. Here they are looking for three distinct requirements:

1. **Difficult Market Entry**
2. **High Margins**
3. **Longevity**

"Your new supermarket project, Mr Bloggs......it certainly has difficult Market Entry and the Margins are at least 12,000 feet......but I have serious doubts about its likely Longevity!"

These aspects are all too often ignored when people assess a new project. They can create problems later on and are worth looking at more closely.

The first requirement, "Difficult Market Entry", seems a contradiction. Why should they want the project to have difficulty getting into the market? The answer lies in the simple fact that as soon as a business starts and appears to others to be successful, it encourages a whole pile of "me-too" imitators who try to jump onto the band-wagon. This causes a dilution of the market and the possibility of price wars etc. Thus it is a considerable advantage to have a project which is not easy for others to copy.

There are a number of barriers which can discourage (or even prevent) a new competitor. These include — specialist skills or knowledge (technical, creative or otherwise); patent protection; licences (some of which may restrict competition); protected niche markets and/or binding contracts with all the main likely customers. What cannot be regarded as a safe barrier against a competitor entering the market is a high capital requirement.

The second requirement, "High Margins", is a fairly obvious requirement as it provides good profitability. But what this also means is that the business should enjoy good positive cashflow, have funds for further development and allow it to survive if margins are reduced by unforeseen events or sales are not up to initial expectations. Just what constitutes a "high" or "low" margin is difficult to say in general terms as it depends on many factors, but refer also to the Chapter **Pricing** and the table on Distribution Channels in the Chapter **Sorting Out The Sales Distribution**.

The final requirement, "Longevity", is not often considered at the planning stage by small businesses as too much emphasis is placed on short-term results. Longevity in this context means a project which once launched is likely to continue to be competitive and profitable for a number of years without substantial change (or further investment), thereby justifying any initial investment to launch the project. Thus "trendy" business ideas are discouraged or those that rely on too many external factors which experience has shown to be volatile (eg international currency exchange fluctuations; oil prices etc).

In conclusion, if the proposed project fails to meet *all* these three criteria, this must be considered as a significant argument against the project and to pursue it further would require very careful consideration indeed.

New Territory If the new project takes the business into new territory — either from a technical or geographical standpoint or there is any other major change, there is considerable risk due simply to your lack of knowledge of what you are going to find. Only very thorough Market Research and preparation might reduce this risk.

THE DETAILED LOOK

If the project looks satisfactory from a broad look, then the next step is to assess the results of the detailed market research. Here we seek to answer two specific questions:
1. Does the project appear to be viable? (If so, what assumptions are being made?).
2. What detailed form should the project take to match the market's requirements.

To allow you to assess as objectively as possible the large amount of market research information gathered, we suggest the "put it down on one sheet of paper" approach. This not only reduces the information to an amount that can be assimilated but it does also encourage you to read through all the information beforehand.

IMPACT ASSESSMENT

Classical Market Research tends to focus attention on assessing the viability of a proposed project. The small business really ought also to consider the project's potential impact on the owner(s) lifestyle and on the business itself. Every new project will have its ups and downs which may have direct consequences for the owner(s) of the business and it might even threaten the original business.

Lifestyle In the early stages of a business, entrepreneur(s) usually have to work long and arduous hours, quite beyond what the average employee would think of as "hard work". In addition some sacrifices may be made and great risks, usually financial, are taken (not only by the entrepreneur(s) but often their families too) — all in an attempt to realise the ambition of creating a successful business.

However, once the early stages are past it is useful to reflect on these lifestyle issues especially the impact any new project might have. In particular, will the new project which is being considered make impossible demands on your time and energy or will it constrain your freedom further? A question to ask yourself is — where do I want to be in 5 year's time and does this new project help me to achieve that? Do I want all the problems of

Assessing A New Project

starting a new venture all over again?

A useful back-of-envelope exercise is to scribble down in two separate columns those aspects of business which you like and those which you dislike. Will the new project enhance the "likes" or increase the "dislikes"?

Business Stability (Unfortunately all too many sound businesses have collapsed due to the launch of a new project which went wrong. Almost every new major project develops completely unforeseen problems and even well-known companies sometimes teeter on the verge of bankruptcy when a project runs into trouble.

You should therefore pause to consider a worst case scenario, quantifying the likely impact on the business if everything goes wrong. It is worth remembering that if the new project runs into problems it will make at least two major and immediate demands on the existing core business,

which are — management time and money! If the original business cannot sustain the loss of those two precious commodities, the whole business will be jeopardised and what might have been a perfectly healthy business could fail.

Some thought should be given to ensuring you have a "back door" or "escape route" prepared in the event of trouble.

On a more positive note the new project could produce spin-offs or utilise unused capacity in the existing business and might even take-off to the point where the original core business is simply allowed to decline and the new project becomes, in time, the principal activity of the business — a type of metamorphosis, a feature of many successful businesses trading today.

Forecasting

None of us tend to be very good at

forecasting the future, the more so the further ahead we attempt to look. From a small business standpoint even looking one year ahead is difficult enough, but it really is essential to make some effort in this respect. Market Research should provide most of the clues. In particular you should note:

1. Trade Trends. Based on statistical information (though these tend to be historic).
2. Trends in the Economy. As it relates to the spending power of your market.
3. Activities of Competitors. In particular, any changes of product or tactics.
4. Analysis of Sales. Probably one of the most important indicators.
5. Weather Trends. Where this affects your business.

This information should be reflected in your Cashflow Forecast and Marketing Plan for the new project■

PRE-PROJECT LAUNCH

Chapters

This Section is entitled "Pre-Project" as activities such as Pricing, Distribution and Image should be thought through in great detail before any new project or venture is launched. These aspects of marketing should *also* be reviewed on a regular basis for existing projects, for the following reasons:

Pricing The different factors which affect your selling price are constantly varying. As this variation is normally upwards, your margins will be cut unless you react.

Distribution One of the opportunities that sometimes presents itself to the alert business is the chance to open up new distribution channels.

Some of the best opportunities come quite unexpectedly and through people you know, so it is worth taking time to cultivate your contacts.

Image A business often starts without a clear concept of what image is most appropriate and gradually over time some sort of image forms but it is unlikely to be co-ordinated. Thus at some early stage you should give this aspect some more thought.

Market Entry & Its Relationship To Pricing etc

The last Chapter in this Section discusses "market entry" which is relevant to any new project or venture.

How you plan to enter a market is inextricably linked to your Pricing, Distribution and Image. This is an important concept to grasp. To understand this better, consider an example of a company that has just produced a new health food and they are trying to work out the best way to market it.

Market Penetration Their first task is to decide which segment of the market may be interested in the new product. In fact there may be more than one — in this case there are health fanatics and general consumers. Next the company has to consider how innovative their product is and how easily it can be copied. The table below will help them choose the price point and required level of promotion.

PRODUCT/SERVICE TYPE 1	PRODUCT/SERVICE TYPE 2
Description: Not innovative; Readily copied; Few competitive advantages. **Object:** Slow Market Penetration **Method:** Low Price, Small Promotion	**Description:** Innovative; Readily copied; Buyers need little educating. **Object:** Fast Market Penetration **Method:** Low Price, Large Promotion
PRODUCT/SERVICE TYPE 3	**PRODUCT/SERVICE TYPE 4**
Description: Innovative; Not easily copied; Buyers need some educating. **Object:** Slow Market Skimming **Method:** High Price, Small Promotion	**Description:** Innovative; Readily copied and/or easy to learn. **Object:** Fast Market Skimming **Method:** High Price, Large Promotion

Product Type 1: Here slow penetration is achieved as the small promotion is so as not to alert potential competitors, and the low price does not allow them to under-cut.

Product Type 2: In this situation the object is to achieve rapid market penetration and domination, thereby leaving little room for a competitor.

Product Type 3: Here one can opt either for a small level of promotion which therefore only skims the potential market or a high level of promotion which does so more quickly.

Product Type 4: If there is a possibility of copying then the slow skimming option above would be less advisable.

In the example of the health food, the company's market research indicated that health fanatics were likely to pay more than general consumers. Hence

assuming the product had some innovations but could be readily copied, the company would have to consider their product was a Type 2 or 4. Both require a large promotion but a Type 4 allows a higher price (better margin) though the disadvantage of allowing a potential competitor to get into the market. The answer might be to start with a high price (aimed at the health fanatics) then reduce the price to aim at the wider consumer market. This transition should be timed to prevent any competitor from developing a similar product and entering the market.

A Pricing Dilemma

As already mentioned there is a danger when pricing too high. You may be creating awareness for your new product or service but if the idea can be copied readily then you are opening the door to a competitor to under-cut your price.

However, pricing too low can be a problem too (not to mention a loss of profits). Though a low price may attract people, consumers often *try* for price but *buy* for quality, ie they may look at the cheapest first but often end up buying something better ∎

Pricing

Introduction
Surprisingly, few small businesses get their pricing right. Or if they do work out a correct price they do not continue to check it regularly and over a period of time price rises from suppliers might seriously erode the profit margin.

The fundamental objective of any pricing policy must be to achieve the maximum profit possible. This is not simply greed but rather an essential objective for the business. Every business needs to meet its many overheads and create some surplus funds to allow for future investment and protect itself from the inevitable ups and downs of trading. Usually the most pressing need is overheads. What are those overheads?

Overheads This refers to business expenditure which is basically constant, ie recurs irrespective of the actual level of trading. Not surprisingly therefore it is also called "Fixed Costs". For instance, rent, rates, most salaries, insurance, heat and light etc are all regarded as Fixed Costs.

Variable Costs In contrast, "Variable" or "Direct Costs" refer to business expenditure which varies directly in relation to the level of trading, for instance the cost of raw materials or stock.

The Significance of Fixed & Variable Costs To fix a price for a product or service, you base it primarily on these *Fixed* and *Variable Costs* so that you can meet them and then make a surplus (or profit) on top. With *Fixed Costs*, it therefore makes a great deal of difference if you sell one item or a hundred items per year or provide a service for one day or a hundred since the entire *Fixed Costs* have to be recovered on those sales. Dividing the *Fixed Costs* by one, a hundred, or whatever, obviously makes a massive difference to the end price.

These *Fixed Costs* are therefore crucial and an elementary error of many businesses (not simply small business) is to have excessively high overheads. In a small business it is of paramount importance that these overheads (ie the *Fixed Costs*) are not only kept to a minimum but time should be set aside to permit a regular check on these costs as they have a nasty habit of creeping upwards.

The important point to grasp in keeping your overheads down is that a saving of even £1000 is pure profit — think how much extra business you would have to generate to make an equivalent amount of profit? Also, a company that runs a tight ship with lean overheads can afford to price competitively and is therefore more likely to secure sales.

It is perhaps not so surprising that businesses are better at controlling their *Variable Costs*. When a supplier raises his prices most businesses take notice and where the rise is unjustified challenge it or find a new supplier. But again, it is worth spending some time to find the cheapest sources of supply provided their *quality* and *delivery* meet your requirements.

PRACTICAL PRICING METHODS
Here we consider 4 popular methods of pricing, which are outlined then expanded in worked examples below:

1. Cost Plus
2. Market Pricing
3. Backward Pricing
4. Time & Materials

Cost Plus In this method, you work out your actual costs and then add a margin so you can draw a wage for yourself. In its various forms, it is the most common pricing method in use but as the worked examples show (over the page) there are pitfalls to avoid.

Market Pricing In this method, your charges attempt to reflect market conditions. In general, if you price low (in relation to market prices) you hope to increase volume sales and thereby achieve a certain annual profit. Alternatively you may price high, make fewer sales but end up with the same profit. In practice it is not that easy to work out which price to opt for, as buyer interest naturally wanes as a price rises. You try to fix a "market price" by close examination of rivals' prices (which effectively set the market) and by a deep understanding of what motivates your customers to pay a certain price for that type of product or service. In any event you ought to do a Cost Plus calculation just to be sure you are making a sensible profit.

If there is no competitor already setting a market price with a rival or similar product or service then it is much harder to assess just what customers are prepared to pay and a little Test Marketing may answer that question. An obvious danger of being a sole player with a premium priced product or service is that it is an open invitation to a new competitor to price below you with a product or service that may be better or simply promoted more strongly than your own.

Backward Pricing This is another variant of "cost plus" pricing. It occurs when you supply a product or service to a major customer who effectively dictates what they are prepared to pay

KEEPING OVERHEADS DOWN

Staff This is usually a business's biggest overhead. Many small businesses have too many secretarial and/or assistant-type staff. You must minimise staffing – by investing in automation and eliminating all unnecessary "work". Simplify work practices! It is often better to employ one high calibre employee than two or three lesser calibre people. This is particularly true where in small businesses you cannot spend much time supervising staff. In addition you must try to increase the productivity of each member of staff by tight control, a comprehensive job description, proper training and realistic incentives.

Premises This can be a big overhead, especially in retailing where prime sites are important. You have to be careful in the selection of premises. Where possible, if you plan to remain for some time in that location, you may consider buying the premises as money spent on a mortgage is usually an *investment.*

Heat & Light These can be more expensive than necessary. Worth checking!

Finance Most businesses have to borrow money but there are nowadays many ways of financing a project or re-financing it to reduce your finance charges. Borrowing too much is known as "over gearing" and the repayments can cripple a business, especially if times get hard or interest rates rise. Excessive stock levels can be one cause of high borrowing.

Insurances It is always worth seeking alternative quotations.

Vehicles/Travel Vehicles are another very expensive overhead where cost savings can be made by a prudent choice of vehicle in the first place, eg the use of a diesel vehicle in preference to petrol if high mileages are likely; purchasing a vehicle that is 9 to 15 months old rather than brand new; sympathetic use of the vehicle and wise selection of the method of financing the purchase. Shopping around for alternative insurance quotations can be revealing. Where use of public transport (eg trains and planes) and hotels are required, some time spent researching the different fare options can make substantial savings!

Phone Bills These are almost always higher than they need to be, due to: a) unnecessary use before 1pm (in the U.K.) when the cheaper rate takes effect; b) long-winded chatty phone conversations and c) use by staff for private calls. To reduce phone bills, you might put a note on each phone "Can it wait till after 1pm?"and you might also put a note by each phone indicating the cost of a 2, 5 and 10 minute call. Other than better discipline when using phones, you might also acquire a fax machine and use that instead as they tend to be much more time (and hence cost) effective. Another idea is to get a phone call-logger – these not only record each call made but also usually indicate the *cost* of a call while you talk, which is guaranteed to make you chat less! Although these devices are not cheap, they can make savings and provide other benefits too.

Sundries Expenses lumped under the general heading of "sundries" covers a multitude of sins, analysis of which often causes a few surprises (and savings).

and then you attempt to tailor your offering to match their price requirement. Many "cost plus" calculations are then performed, varying the ingredients to see if the usually tough demands of the customer can be met and still leave room to make some profit.

Time & Materials This is common for many non-retail service businesses. The customer is charged for the time spent on a job plus the materials consumed or fitted. The white-collar version of this pricing method is to charge a "Fee plus Expenses". With these pricing methods it is easy to make mistakes either by charging too low an hourly rate or not including all the materials used (including wastage) or expenses incurred.

Time spent travelling to/from the customer and time spent waiting at a customer's premises can again throw out the calculations. If these are likely to be significant then the customer should be made aware that travel and/or waiting time will be charged.

Many people charge materials "at cost" on their invoices. You should be wary of charging for materials at what you paid for them because there are hidden costs which you are ignoring such as the time you take to find and buy the materials, the cost of materials held in stock (ie the overdraft charges on the stock you have paid for, and storage costs), the cost of travel to pick up the materials, etc. Some businesses therefore define "at cost" as the retail price whereas they purchase at wholesale prices, giving themselves a sensible margin.

Pricing

Calculating A Labour Cost

Before looking at how to apply the above pricing methods, we need to take a look at the tricky area of costing labour as it represents an important part of the pricing equation. Two common errors are either to ignore the Proprietor's own time or to ignore the cost of the non-productive time spent by the Proprietor and his or her staff.

a) If you are a one-man operation, then you ought to use a labour rate at least equivalent to that you would have to pay an employee to do the job. This is for two reasons: first, if the business expands and you take on someone, then if your selling price is based on an artificially low labour rate then you will either have to suddenly raise your prices or reduce your profits, which are both undesirable. And second, though you may never consider expanding or taking on staff, if you are working for a labour rate considerably under that which you would offer an employee, then perhaps you are not doing yourself any favours?

A small "cheat" which you may permit yourself in this context is to consider all your evening and week-end work as 'free'. It works like this – use an hourly labour rate equivalent to at least what you would pay an employee and the number of hours such an employee would work in a week. One then considers those hours to be fully productive when doing any calculations. The "cheating" of course is that all the administration and sales work then has to be done effectively "free" in all those extra hours a self-employed person normally works.

b) As for non-productive time, this is particularly apparent when you employ anyone (as they are not going to work overtime 'free' like you!). This non-productive time occurs for many reasons such as holidays and sickness, and more frequently during the course of ordinary work – such as waiting for spare parts to arrive; cleaning the workplace; doing essential paperwork; having to wait at a customer's premises; spending time buying parts or raw materials and so on.

For most situations (excluding charging on a "time & materials" basis, which is covered opposite) as a rough rule of thumb, it is useful to add one third to a half to the basic labour cost, ie if paying someone £200 per week for a 40 hour week, then add 33% to 50% to get a labour rate of £6.65-£7.50 per hour. This addition also allows for the Employers National Insurance Contribution. Note that in the above example, the figure of £6.65-£7.50 does not allow for any profit but merely tries to reflect the actual cost of hiring staff.

c) When charging on a "time & materials" basis, a much more precise calculation of hourly labour rate is necessary. See the worked example on the opposite page under "Pricing Services".

But first we shall look at the pricing of Products.

PRICING PRODUCTS

A straightforward way to price a product is as follows:

1. If you are a manufacturer (This also applies to businesses such as catering where food products are made):

Selling price/unit =
(cost of raw material + direct labour + o/heads contribution) + mark-up + VAT

Let us look at each of these in turn:

Cost of raw material: This should be relatively easy to calculate, but do remember wastage. *Direct labour:* This is the realistic cost of employing staff to make the units, as can be seen in the following example. *Overhead contribution:* This considers the overheads of the business, which obviously have to be supported by the production. It assumes everything that is manufactured is subsequently sold (an important point) and is calculated simply as:

$$\text{Overhead contribution} = \frac{\text{total overheads}}{\text{total production}}$$

Mark-up: The mark-up (see also page 36) is such that the manufactured items can be sold at sufficient profit to cover the proprietor's or Director's wages *plus* a small surplus (say 5-10%) to provide funds for future expansion, new product development or simply to save against any future contingencies. *VAT:* This is only added if you are registered for VAT and the product itself is VAT rated.

Example The following example illustrates some other aspects when using this simplified approach. Assume you produce a small electronic device or craft product and employ one production person, spending most of your own time on sales, fault finding, handling customer enquiries and working on future designs. Assume each item takes 1 hour to assemble, test and package up. Then in a 40 hour week you could make 40 such devices. Assume too the raw materials cost £10. Now, if the employee's wage is

£200 per week, then to start with you could say the direct labour cost per unit made is £200/40 + 33% = £6.65.

Next assume total overheads (ie rent, rates, insurance, phone, lighting, essential travel) come to £12,000 and annual production = 40 units/week x 48 weeks = 1,920 (48 weeks allows for some holidays), then the overhead contribution per unit = £12,000/1,920 = £6.25. Hence the production cost/unit = £10 + £6.65 + £6.25 = £22.90.

Now assume you hope to be able to draw a wage of £10,000 per annum, then this would add a further £10,000/1,920 = £5.20 to each unit, making a total of £28.10. You might then consider a selling price of £28.95 or £29.95 to give you a small surplus profit. In this example, since the annual turnover (ie sales) = 1,920 x £29.95 = £57,504 which is above the current VAT threshold then the business needs to be VAT registered and VAT needs to be added to the cost (assuming the product is VAT rated).

Once a price is calculated it is vital to see how this relates to other prices in the market. See also the points below.

2. If you are a wholesaler or retailer:

Selling price/unit = net cost price + mark-up + VAT (where applicable)

Example If you buy an article for £4.65 net (ie without VAT added) and if the typical mark-up is 85% then the selling price = £4.65 + 85% + VAT which equals £10.11 (if the VAT rate is 17.5% and you are registered for VAT).

As with any selling price but particularly so in the competitive area of retailing, once you have worked out your selling price using the equation you should then consider:

a) ***Psychological Price Barriers*** £1, £5, £10, £20, £50, £100 are all psychological price barriers (they tend to reflect the steps in bank notes). So in the above example it would be better to price it at £9.99 or £9.95.

b) ***Comparative Shopping*** You must know your competitors' prices for similar (or worse still, identical) items. This may force your price down or may allow you to float it up slightly.

c) ***RRP/RSP*** With several notable exceptions, it is illegal for manufacturers to fix retail prices but they frequently have "recommended" retail prices (RRP) or selling prices (RSP), which gives a good guide as to your retail price.

d) ***Loss-Leaders*** Retailers sometimes select one popular product, price it low, then display it prominently in their window (or adverts) to draw customers into their store.

e) ***Image*** A final, complex and sometimes fairly crazy aspect of pricing is the image a price can convey. When other indicators are absent, people too often judge the quality of something by its price, ie when faced with a choice, they will often consider the more expensive one must be better! Conversely, they may not purchase an item because the price seems too cheap.

PRICING SERVICES

The pricing of non-retail services is based normally on time plus materials. To start with you might simply consider the Labour Cost (as discussed above) to which a profit margin (and VAT if appropriate) is added. However, since the figure you use for labour is critical, it might be better to calculate the Labour Cost more accurately. The basic Cost Plus equation then becomes:

$$\text{Hourly Rate} = \frac{\text{total overheads (incl all wages)}}{\text{total likely productive hours}} + \text{mark-up} + \text{VAT}$$

Since the success of the business will be dependent on the accuracy of this figure, it is useful to keep a record of time-utilisation, so that you can begin to get a more accurate feel for this figure. This is even more important if you are tendering for fixed-price contracts, where the profitability is dependent on knowing just how much time it takes to do a particular type of job. The normal means of recording these times are Job Cards which you and your staff need to complete conscientiously.

Example Consider a small car servicing/repair business run by two partners with no employees. Assume their premises rent & rates, phone, heating, lighting and insurance comes to £25,000. Assume also the two partners each draw £12,000 a year and their basic productive week is 40 hours (paperwork and cleaning etc being over and above this). They take 3 weeks holiday per year. The equation, assuming a 10% mark-up would then be:

$$\text{Hourly Rate} = \frac{£25,000 + £12,000 + £12,000}{2 \times (40\text{hrs} \times 49\text{weeks})} + 10\% + \text{VAT}$$

$$= £13.75 + \text{VAT}$$

Once the Hourly Rate is calculated, then by checking this against what competitors are charging, you could work backwards to see what profit margin was possible. Note this business would also make a profit on the parts it uses.

Pricing

MARGIN, MARGIN . . . .
. . . . ALWAYS MARGIN

The astute business person knows the vital importance of maintaining the profit margins. What is less frequently realised is that a few percentage points on a mark-up can make a worthwhile percentage increase in *profits*.

The normally accepted definition of mark-up is:

$$\text{Mark-up} = \frac{\text{selling price - cost price}}{\text{cost price}} \times 100\%$$

And margin is normally defined as:

$$\text{Margin} = \frac{\text{selling price - cost price}}{\text{selling price}} \times 100\%$$

THE E-FACTOR

Once you have carried out any formalised pricing using the equations mentioned above, then consider what might be called the "E-Factor", as in **Extra**. This is an additional mark-up which can propel a firm's meagre profit performance into something creditable or even help to rescue a firm which is not doing too well. Intuitive entre-preneurs usually do this, almost sub-consciously, but it is rarely mentioned in theoretical treatises on pricing. This is possibly because it is more of a concept which you can apply in a number of subtle ways than a rigid formula or procedure.

Another way of thinking about or justifying the E-Factor is to consider it as an extra element in your pricing to allow for contingencies which would otherwise adversely affect your overall profitability. Such a need arises for many different reasons. These are situations such as: suppliers whose invoices turn out to be much higher than their original estimates or the little (or not so little) items you forgot to include in your own estimates, eg the extra cost of having to return faulty or incorrect goods; the unexpected time spent on fixed price jobs; the delays in clearing goods through Customs, and so on.

The E-Factor can be applied in many different ways:

Variable Mark-ups As any good retailer knows you need to search constantly for lower-than-normal priced merchandise which can be sold for a similar price as other similar quality products but with scope for a higher profit margin. The idea of variable mark-ups can be adopted by most types of business. A firm providing a number of services should price them differently (ie varying the mark-up) depending on what the market can stand. And a firm which makes or supplies a range of products should also mark them up differently. The key is *flexibility*, but always seeking the maximum possible margin.

A practice which is not recommended, is to offer the same product or service to two different customers for two different prices, unless you can justify this by the quantity being purchased or some other sensible reason.

Incorporate All Expenses When invoicing a customer, remember to include all the additional expenses associated with that particular sale and which are justifiable, eg postage or freight charges, phone calls, currency changes etc. Even if you are selling a piece of equipment or providing a service with a value of over £1,000, it might at first glance seem a bit mean to add on a further £10 or whatever — but if it is justifiable and fair then you not only ought to add this, but you need to do so.

Reflect Any Changes If you have provided a written quotation and the customer makes changes which involve you spending more time or using more materials or whatever, this extra cost should be reflected in your final invoice. (Note: Your Standard Quotation should include a clause which allows you to do this).

A common occurrence is when you are asked to provide a quotation which you do on the basis of performing the work within a "normal" timescale. The purchaser then delays his or her decision until the eleventh hour and then wants you to respond almost immediately. In attempting to do this you usually incur additional expenses and these ought to be passed on to the customer. There is sometimes a reluctance to do this especially if you are trying to woo a new or important customer but people rarely question a fair charge. (If they do grumble about it then maybe they are not worth doing business with!).

Premium Pricing This is being able to supply a product (not so common with services) at a premium price. This situation occurs when demand far exceeds supply and the product (or service) has a degree of exclusivity and cannot be copied readily. It is characterised by long customer waiting lists.

ESTIMATES & QUOTATIONS

An "estimate" is the approximate price of something, but usually a buyer will ask for a "quotation" and in writing. A quotation is a fixed price and if agreed is binding on both parties. See opposite.

TRING - A - LING
A·L·A·R·M·S

Tel: 071-123 456

**Number Ten
Sellers Lane
London EC1**

Mr A McSwindle
General Manager
Worthless Products Ltd
Unit 3, Industrial Estate
BIRMINGHAM   B1 1ZZ

14th June 1990

Dear Mr McSwindle

WINDOW GRILLES - QUOTATION

As a result of our meeting yesterday I have pleasure in providing you with the following quotation to supply and fit window grilles for your factory.

Quantity.   Four windows - all to rear of premises facing railway line.

Specification.   Mild steel expanded mesh as per sample left with you.
Mesh to be fastened to window surrounds by masonry nails.

Price.   The total is £639.00 + VAT. This quotation is valid for 30 days.

Terms.   Payment is due 30 days from date of Invoice.

Guarantee.   We guarantee our workmanship and materials for 12 months.

If you have any questions, please do not hesitate to call me. I look forward to hearing from you in the near future.

Yours sincerely

A. Bell

A Bell
Sales Manager

Partners: A. Bell, A. Clanger

Fictitious example

Pricing

DISCOUNTING

The opposite to the E-Factor is to discount. The only reasons for discounting are to encourage sales or early payment. The circumstances under which discounting can be used vary widely. They include:

a) Launching a new product or service. You might offer a "come and try it" discount to encourage early customer acceptance.

b) Selling off obsolete stock. This not only allows space for new stock and helps cashflow but hopefully catches some customers before the stock is too obsolete to be sold at all.

c) Selling perishable stock as it approaches the end of its shelf-life.

d) Encouraging the customer to order a larger quantity than he might otherwise do.

e) Clinching a sale. (See comment below).

f) Matching (or Undercutting) a competitor. (See comment below).

g) Early payment. Where dealing with trade customers who expect credit terms, a small discount (eg 2.5%) can be offered if payment is made within a specified period (eg 30 days).

These seven situations above are all good reasons for discounting. There is of course an eighth situation which is less healthy where a business discounts to increase volume sales because of cashflow problems or to bolster flagging sales figures. The retail sector has seen a lot of this in recent years.

Clinching A Sale It is a very common (and successful) tactic to close a sale by offering a discount to a potential customer who is wavering. It is normally on the basis of "x% off if you decide right here and now". Such discounts can range from 5% to 15% but may sometimes go further (though this may make a buyer wonder how big a mark-up the supplier is putting on in the first place to afford such generous discounts!).

In a trade context, to keep your credibility and to maintain your prices for the future, you need to dream up some excuse for the discount, eg an introductory offer to a new buyer; a special promotion on a new product; a discount for all orders taken during a Trade Show, and so on.

Matching/Undercutting Where you discount prices as a result of competitor action, it needs to be done with extreme caution. Not only does it diminish your precious margins but it may trigger a "price war" — see the Chapter **Coping With Competitors**.

A final point on the subject of discounting is that continuous or regular discounting or "Sales" teaches your customers bad habits. If you always have a "Sale" at a certain time of the year they may delay their purchasing until then. A more insidious aspect is regular discounting reduces the perceived "correct" market price for your product or service so your normal prices suddenly appear expensive ■

---

7 Common Errors When Pricing

1. Not taking into account the true value of your own time.
2. Not comparing actual costs incurred with the invoiced price, to ensure the correct margin was achieved and to reflect this in future quotations.
3. Forgetting to increase prices in line with inflation.
4. Being afraid to put the correct and full price on your product or service.
5. Discounting too much, too often.
6. Not reacting to changes which occur in a competitor's prices.
7. Thinking the customer is only concerned with price.

Sorting Out The Sales Distribution

Introduction

Although this particular Chapter is aimed primarily at manufacturers, importers and wholesalers of products, it may also be relevant to firms who regard themselves as being in the service sector but who have a tangible product to sell. For example, a computer software company may opt to sell its software packages direct to the end user or choose to distribute them through intermediaries.

Deciding which distribution channel, or channels, to use is an on-going problem that confronts almost every manufacturer, importer and wholesaler. It is all very well having a superb product to offer but sorting out the way to distribute the most at the best prices can be critical to the success of the venture.

Manufacturers sometimes resent the mark-up which the wholesalers or retailers are putting on their goods, while wholesalers complain about poor deliveries from suppliers and the extended credit retailers often take.

Some small manufacturers or importers are sometimes tempted to market their products directly but the cost of this can be prohibitive.

There is no simple yet *ideal* distribution channel, as each has its own complications, advantages and disadvantages. A business may use a variety of methods concurrently or may use different methods in different geographical areas.

Shown over page are the main distribution options.

Piggy Back One neat method of distributing your product is if you can ride piggy back on another, usually larger, company's distribution system. An example might be to approach another company who has a large salesforce on the road selling products to similar buyers as your own but whose products are not in direct competition. Another example might be to tag onto someone else's mail order catalogue. The method is not always feasible of course, but it is well worth thinking about.

Joint Venture One good way for a small business to expand its sales is to team up with another similar small business operating in another part of the country or who have different customers.

Which Distribution Channel?

Depending upon which distribution channel you choose the margins can vary dramatically from a seemingly paltry 5-15% if you are an intermediary (ie importer, wholesaler or agent) to maybe considerably more if selling directly. But, and this is the big "but", almost invariably those distribution options which have the higher margins also carry proportionally higher overheads and so the actual profitability is often not so dissimilar!

You should therefore decide on a distribution channel(s) for reasons other than simply margin. See the Table overpage.

Trial & Error

If there appears no obviously best way to distribute your products then a degree of trial and error may be needed. However, you must try to avoid any conflict of interest with your existing customers.

Conflict of Interest

Although you may start with one particular distribution channel there may be a temptation to try others as well. In that event you need to ensure that any new channel is not going to make you lose your original customers. For instance, if you were selling to retailers and then you decided to launch mail-order too (which might lead to the retailers losing customers), then you would soon be in trouble, some retailers simply cancelling or reducing their orders and selecting from other suppliers. In that particular case the problem could probably be avoided by offering slightly different products for mail-order, or if they are the same then ensuring that they are at least at a similar price to what retailers are selling them for and then *adding* any post and packaging.

Another conflict of interest can occur when you supply a firm and are then approached by a similar firm who are competitors to the first. In some trades it is common practice for a manufacturer to supply almost anyone who can buy their products irrespective of competition between their customers. In other trades, people tend to be supplied on a more exclusive basis.

Whenever you plan to embark on a course of action that is likely to upset (or lose) existing customers it is obviously prudent to take their views into consideration.

Using Agents

Many small companies who cannot afford full-time Sales Representatives use Agents who sell on commission. These are self-employed salespeople who usually carry several non-competing product lines. The Agent merely takes orders, with delivery, invoicing (and chasing bad payers) normally being the responsibility of the supplier. Finding good Agents can be very difficult. Agents sometimes appear dilatory, their efforts seem minimal and their paperwork may be incomplete. However

Sorting Out The Sales Distribution

to be fair to Agents, the 10%-15% commission they earn on the sales from a small company can often amount to very little. Furthermore some of their companies either do not deliver the goods ordered or worse still they do not pay the commission due to their Agents!

Agents need to be selected with care, preferably on recommendation. They should have contacts, experience of the trade and should not carry so many lines that they cannot look after your product adequately. Agents should be given your full backing and support (just as if they were partners in your business) and their work should be monitored carefully. Commission would normally be paid on the net sales (ie after discounts) and when invoiced rather than when the customer pays. All these details should be covered in a written Agreement.

This Agreement should include the following points: a) *Commission* to be paid (normally expressed as a percentage) and when this will be paid; b) *Geographical Area* in which the Agent can operate. In particular it needs to be agreed if commission is earned on sales made by customers in that area placing orders directly (normally commission is due on *all* sales from a given area); c) *Authority* of the Agent to negotiate different prices/delivery terms etc; d) *Termination* ie the period of notice required by both sides to end the Agreement.

Retailers Have Options Too

Retailers who usually consider themselves at the end of the product distribution chain may in fact have a few distribution options to consider themselves. For instance they can open further outlets under their own management; open franchised outlets; open shops-within-shops; use agents to sell by party-plan and so on. So even they can and should give "distribution" some thought.

DIRECT MARKETING

Mail Order, Direct Mail, most Mailshots, Party Plan Selling and Multi-level Marketing are all examples of Direct Marketing where the wholesaler and retailer are cut out from the sales distribution chain. Direct Marketing uses the post, the phone, direct-response advertising and personal contact to find its customers. Direct Marketing can be a suitable means for making sales to both consumers and business customers and it has seen a rapid increase in popularity in the past two decades.

MAIL ORDER

We are all familiar with the traditional large mail order catalogues. More recently there has been a rise in the number of small specialist catalogues, sometimes called "specialogues", which focus on one popular area — fashion, gifts, books, a particular hobby or sport, etc. These are all examples of mail order, where the customers browse through the catalogues in the comfort of their homes then place their orders (over 60% do so by phone) and get delivery of the goods, normally on a sale-or-return basis, within 28 days. In almost every case payment can be by cheque or credit card and with the large mail order companies there is credit available (nearly one quarter of all British adults have some sort of mail order credit commitment).

The large catalogues survive and thrive because they act rather like a department store but with the added convenience and privacy of purchasing in one's own home. Their offer of extended credit gave them a significant marketing advantage over the High Street retailers until the more recent expansion of retail credit. Most of the products on show in these huge catalogues can be purchased at similar prices in the High Street.

In contrast, the much smaller specialist catalogues survive *mainly* because what they are offering is not readily available from shops. In fact many of the products they show are unique to them, often possessing some novelty value.

For a small business this uniqueness is essential in any mail order selling. If a customer can purchase the same (or similar) product readily elsewhere it is unlikely your promotion will succeed.

Another popular form of mail order is selling "off-the-page" as it is called. Here, instead of producing a catalogue, the business places an advertisement usually offering one or a limited number of products for sale.

To protect the consumer when ads ask for money in advance of the goods being delivered, there are a number of Mail Order Protection Schemes (MOPS). The largest is that run by the National Newspapers and they carefully assess new mail order businesses and their products before the mail order ads are accepted. Obtain further information from MOPS, 16 Took's Court, London EC4A 1LB. Tel: 071-405 6806.

DIRECT MAIL

Whereas Mail Order has a passive sales element to it, ie the customer receives a catalogue or sees an advertisement and may or may not respond, direct mail is, as its name suggests, more direct. It can be used for consumers or business

DISTRIBUTION CHANNELS

CHANNEL	SETTING-UP COSTS	MARKET COVERAGE	MANAGEMENT	MARGINS	COMMENTS
1. SELLING THROUGH INTERMEDIARIES, ie Wholesalers, Mail Order companies or to other manufacturers (where one is supplying a component). (Excludes retailers)	A cheap option, as you are dealing with relatively few clients so you can do the sales yourself or with your own sales people. However in certain trades the intermediaries are noted for being slow payers which increases your set up cash needs dramatically.	The ultimate coverage can be very wide, though you need to check the capabilities of the intermediaries in this respect.	Relatively straightforward to manage.	Very dependent on the particular trade. Tend not to be high but neither are the o/heads (relative to other parts of the distribution chain).	This, or Option 2, is the route many manufacturers take. If cash or management resources are limited this would be the option to consider first.
2. SELLING THROUGH INTERMEDIARIES, ie Retailers, or where the number of Intermediaries is much larger than Option 1.	If using your own salesforce this option will be more expensive than Option 1 as there are more customers to service. But if you use self-employed Agents on a commission basis it might be even cheaper than Option 1.	Coverage may be better than Option 1, but not necessarily.	Larger client base will inevitably make bigger demands on management time.	As the wholesaler is missed out the margin will be more than Option 1 but so are overheads. The larger client base spreads your credit risk.	This is a popular option – might be considered when there are either no suitable wholesalers or their coverage is poor.
3. SELLING DIRECT TO END-USER (Trade)	Similar to Option 1 or 2.	Could be very comprehensive.	Relatively straightforward to manage.	Margins are often dictated by the end-user and may be pared to the bone by a large customer.	If you make parts or equipment for other firms, you may need to sell direct to them.
4. SELLING DIRECT TO END-USER (Consumer) by DIRECT MAIL or MAIL ORDER	Adverts & leaflets are both expensive. Extra staff may be needed to handle orders and storage of goods also needs thought. Not a cheap option!	The degree of coverage directly relates to cash available for promotion. A small budget needs a highly targetted approach.	Ditto.	Margins maximised as you sell at retail prices, but high costs of promotion can erode profits quickly.	This is always a tempting option — "Getting rid of the middle-man" but its difficult and costly to do successfully.
5. SELLING DIRECT TO END-USER (Consumer) by PARTY PLAN or MLM ("Direct Selling")	Setting-up costs are some-where between Option 2 and Option 4.	Could, ultimately, be very comprehensive but likely to start small.	Management workload is probably similar to Option 2.	Margins may be maxi-mised as you are selling at near-retail prices but the associated o/heads can be less than retailing.	This is a very specialised option which is only appropriate for certain products.
6. SELLING DIRECT TO END-USER (Consumer) through OWN RETAIL OUTLETS	If the shops are company owned then setting-up costs are high. Another approach is to have franchised outlets.	Coverage limited to your outlet(s) which, realistically, is likely to be a small %-age of the possible market.	This option needs a larger management team as you are running 2 quite different businesses.	Having your own outlets allows more control of prices and margins (within the constraints of the wider market).	Altho' this is not a common approach it has several advantages assuming you have the cash and management team.

Sorting Out The Sales Distribution

customers. Its strength (and weakness) lies in the quality of the mailing list on which the mailshot is based.

Direct Mail is particularly useful for selling to existing customers whose details (ie name and address) you have on record. Note that if you are going to keep information relating to individuals on a computer, even if it is just names and addresses, then you will normally need to register under the Data Protection Act (costs currently £75 for 3 years). For further information contact the Registrar's Enquiry Service. Tel: Wilmslow (0625) 535777.

Mailing Lists   Here are three ways of acquiring a mailing list: a) you can produce your own list; b) you can purchase a list or c) you can rent one. If you compile your own you probably need a PC computer with suitable software if the number of names and addresses exceeds 100 or so. You can list the names and the addresses of existing customers or find new ones by your own research using Directories such as the Yellow Pages.

An alternative is to purchase a mailing list. The cost of this depends entirely on the quality of the list you purchase. Prices are normally quoted in terms of £ per hundred or thousand names. A common problem with most mailing lists is they suffer from duplicates and obsolete names or addresses, ie some of the names and addresses you will be buying will be simply rubbish.

Due to the time and effort necessary to maintain a good quality mailing list it is becoming more common to "rent" a mailing list. In this situation you never see the list as it is sent to an independent mailing house which will stick the labels onto your envelopes. In this way the owner of the list does not risk it being copied and you can make use of it for much less cost than outright purchase. "BRAD Direct Marketing" is a directory listing over 4,000 business and consumer mailing lists available for rental (see BRAD's address on page 59).

Socio-Economic Groups   With consumer mailing lists, (and in some publications' details of their readership) you might come across references to consumers as being AB, C1 etc. These refer to a scheme of grading consumers as follows: A = Upper middle class (ie senior executives and professionals); B = Middle class; C1 = Lower middle class (ie clerical, junior management); C2 = Skilled working class manual workers; D = Working class (ie semi or unskilled workers) and E = people with the lowest incomes.

Consumers   Whereas business mailing lists can be compiled in a relatively straightforward manner, consumers are more difficult to classify. However there is one powerful system called ACORN (which stands for "A Classification Of Residential Neighbourhoods") which classifies all neighbourhoods into 38 types such as "Private Houses Well-off Elderly" or "Recent Council Estates" etc. Then working on the not unreasonable assumption that people who live in similar neighbourhoods have similar lifestyles and spending habits, one can produce some very interesting mailing lists. For more information contact your local Royal Mail Sales Representative. You can also discuss the Royal Mail's other services including Freepost and door-to-door distribution of circulars.

PARTY PLAN/MULTILEVEL MARKETING
Party Plan and Multi-level Marketing (MLM) are also called "shopping at home" or "Direct Selling". MLM is when distributors involved in selling the products gain bonuses from the sales of other distributors they appoint under them. This is also called networking. In 1990, Direct Selling accounted for sales of three quarters of a billion pounds. Most companies are members of the Direct Selling Association who have a Code of Practice. For further information contact them at 29, Floral Street, London WC2E 9DP, tel: 071-497 1234.

SOME LEGALITIES
The general advertisement legalities discussed at the end of the Chapter **Advertising – How?** apply to more than just ads in publications. Mail order (and direct mail) advertisers also need to show their full name and address together with the delivery time (eg "allow ... days for delivery" and this period should not exceed 28 days).

Note also the provisions of the Consumer Protection Act and the Cancellation of Contracts Concluded away from Business Premises Regulations, further details of which can be provided by your local Trading Standards Officer.

EXPORTING

Why Export?   Businesses start to export for different reasons, such as the desire to make the most of a good product or service which is applicable to a wider market than just the UK. Another reason is as a precaution in case there is a downturn in the UK economy. A less good reason might be to try selling something abroad because it is not selling well enough in the UK.

Some companies actively pursue an export policy and produce a Marketing Plan with that venture in mind, while other companies slip into exporting because they have been approached by an overseas buyer and this slowly leads to other export sales.

Government, naturally enough, tries to encourage exports, but the proprietor of a small business cannot afford to be dazzled by the sales pitch. Also, though there is much promotion of the European Single Market, there are of course many important markets outwith Europe, notably North America. As a small business it may be wise to focus initially on one small export area, possibly only *part* of one country, rather than trying to take on the whole world!

Who Should Think of Exporting? First of all, a small company should probably not consider exporting unless either the company is well established in its home market making it financially strong enough to set out on this new adventure or one of the proprietors has been in this field before and "knows the ropes". This therefore does not exclude new or recently started businesses.

Exporting can be exciting, though the initial glamour of jetting around the world and staying in hotels etc can wear thin. It certainly can provide enormous opportunities even for the smallest of businesses – provided they have the right things to sell.

Exporting, however, is not something just to dabble in!

GETTING INTO EXPORT

Market Research As with any new business venture, the first thing to do is to find out more about the market, ie to do some market research. There are people who can help (speak to your Enterprise Agency or business development unit), but one good and quick way is to visit an appropriate trade show in the country concerned. Speak to people in the trade over there and get copies of relevant foreign trade publications (to translate selected articles later).

It may be that your product will require modifying to suit specific overseas markets. Find out too if you need an import licence for the country concerned, if there are any import duties and if you require an export licence from the UK (such licences are needed only for a limited range of items).

Distribution Assuming your market research results are encouraging, for manufacturers the next decision to make is how to market your product. The conventional distribution alternatives are as follows:

1. Agent. An agent will visit potential customers and take orders, usually on a 10% commission. You then ship the

---

SOME ADVANTAGES OF EXPORTING

Market Size Obviously one of the biggest advantages is the potential market is larger than simply this country.

Market Match The product or service you are selling might suit certain overseas markets better than the UK.

Eggs in several baskets Selling in export markets may provide a possible "hedge" against recession in this economy.

Currency Advantage Although outwith your control, a change in exchange rates can give you an advantage if Sterling is weak against your customer's currency.

SOME DISADVANTAGES OF EXPORTING

High Costs It's very expensive travelling abroad to get orders. Expensive in management time too. It's also expensive shipping goods and paying Agent's fees which raises your prices and may make them uncompetitive.

Market Mismatch Culture, customs and language can all be different to what you are used to – sometimes quite alien. This has the practical problem that a successful product or service in the UK might be of little use or interest to people abroad.

Regulations You need to know what local regulations apply and if there are import restrictions or onerous duties.

Shipping Procedures There is a lot to learn!

Currency Disadvantage Just as a change in exchange rates can be beneficial, equally it might not be!

Unpaid Debts A potential problem facing businesses which export is collecting debts. This can be a very serious problem.

---

goods direct to the customer and invoice these customers direct. The main problems here are finding a good, reliable agent and controlling customer debt.

2. Distributor. A distributor not only goes out taking orders but also keeps stock of your goods. You then only have to ship goods to the distributor and invoice them. As with agents, they should not only sell your goods but also provide important feedback from customers.

You could find an agent or distributor by recommendation through your trade association or from another British company. Alternatively the DTI (Department of Trade and Industry) operate the "Export Representative Service" which for a fee will provide a list of businesses in the country concerned who may be interested in representing your firm.

Sorting Out The Sales Distribution

3. Sell Direct. This can be done by taking a Stand at a Trade Show abroad and hopefully taking orders direct from individual customers. But before that, it is worth going just as a visitor to assess the Show and the competition.

After taking orders at a Show, follow-up sales might be difficult or just too expensive for you to undertake, but if you attend the Trade Shows regularly, customers will come to expect to see you there.

If you plan to make your contacts through an annual overseas Trade Show, a good rule-of-thumb is: the first year you will not make enough sales to cover your costs, the second year you may, with luck, break even and in the third year you *may* achieve profit.

4. Collaborative Projects. A completely different approach is some form of collaboration with an overseas company. This might take the form of you providing certain facilities or contacts for them in exchange for them providing the same for you. Or you may consider a joint venture or licensing arrangement with such a company.

Services: The above options have been listed with a manufacturer in mind. For a service based business, the options depend very much on the type of business concerned.

Pricing A major problem with exports is the extra costs that need to be built-in which inevitably make your products more expensive abroad than they would be if selling at home. Even if you are selling on an "ex-factory" or "fob" basis, the end price of the goods will still be higher. (*Note:* "fob" means "free on board", ie your price includes carriage to and loading on board the plane, ship or truck at an agreed UK port).

The additional costs of exporting include freight charges (and the often onerous handling and shipping agent fees); shipping insurance; export credit insurance; import duties where applicable and bank charges. There might also be your overseas agent's commission to add.

Hence a product which can retail in the UK for, say £10 (with a 100% mark-up for the retailer) might be the equivalent of £12, £15 or more, on the shelves in another country. This can obviously diminish the appeal of your product unless the foreign economy can withstand the higher price or if the currency conversion is in your favour.

How To Send Goods For most products there are probably three options. The first option (if the goods are lightweight) is by post. This can be by air (which is relatively expensive but quick) or surface (which is cheaper but takes many weeks to most places). One big advantage is that you have no handling agent's fees, so for small orders this can be quite useful.

However, most exporters will have to consider using the two other options – air freight or sea freight. A good Shipping Agent is essential to handle the often complicated documentation and to advise on the best route and carrier – the most direct way is not always the best. If you are quoted a shipping cost in terms of £/kg (quite often its $/kg), then remember to ask about the handling charges which can add quite a lot to the overall bill.

ARRANGING PAYMENT

It is one thing to succeed in getting an export order, it is quite another matter to actually get paid for it! Certain countries seem to be notorious non-payers while others have the reputation of being excellent payers. Expert advice is needed and this is available from the DTI's Export Credits Guarantee Department, 2 Exchange Tower, Harbour Exchange Square, London E14 9GS, tel: 071-512 7000.

Whereas with a UK customer you might insist on payment by proforma (ie they pay before you send the goods) the normal method for an unknown export customer is to use either a Letter of Credit or other documentary collection, which are handled through your bank and are relatively safe.

If you plan to offer credit, then do remember to take up references just as you would do with any UK customer.

Note that a bank will charge not only to arrange the transfer of cash (by eg Letter of Credit) but will also charge to convert a foreign currency payment into Sterling. To avoid the latter you could ask your customer if they can pay by "Sterling cheque drawn on a UK bank" – and if they are unable to do this then ask your bank what their conversion charges are likely to be.

GETTING MORE ADVICE

Exporting is very exciting and can provide enormous opportunities. However it also presents potential pitfalls for the unwary and too many small companies get their fingers burnt in the process. If you are seriously considering exporting, as a first step you might speak to an expert provided through the government's "Enterprise Initiative". Phone: 0800 500 200 for a free booklet.

In terms of "Business In Europe", there is further literature available from government, tel: 0272 444 888.

Finally, your local Chamber of Commerce or Enterprise Agency might run an Exporters Club■

It might be thought that "image" is only something which large corporations need be concerned with. Certainly, such corporations are very image conscious and they seem to spend a great deal of money and effort on this. To a small firm, it can even sound a bit grand when all you want to do is get out there and make a few sales! The cynics might also ask why anyone should take the trouble — after all, if the customer is getting the right product or service at the right price, where does "image" enter the picture?

In a simple Utopian world with no competition and uncluttered by human beings with their complex emotions, preconceptions, prejudices, dreams and delusions, "image" might indeed be irrelevant. But in the real world it most certainly is relevant and every business, large or small, projects an image whether it is a good one or not and whether it is done consciously or not. Accordingly it might as well be done as professionally as possible.

Image might be thought of as the personality or character of a product or service made up from both physical and emotional factors. Image adds to the value of a product or service as perceived by the customer. It gives an aura that differentiates it from others and makes it more desirable than products or services of a basically similar nature.

In fact, if the right image is projected, it might just give a customer the confidence to buy from a small, and possibly still newish, firm.

To get an idea of the sort of image other businesses are projecting, ask yourself, for instance, where would you go to buy a cheap runabout car? Would you visit a large main car dealer on a prestige site with carpeted showrooms,

sales staff in grey suits and coffee machines just for their customers? Probably not — they are putting over a more up-market image. Instead you might buy the car from a secondhand car dealer operating from a muddy site, the salesmen wearing grubby anoraks and the only coffee being that available from a vacuum flask! Here you would expect to find cheaper cars (but would generally expect fewer guarantees with what you buy).

Another example to consider is where you buy your clothes and what it is that draws you to some shops in preference to others. Is it their convenience? Fashion sense? Good prices? Known brand names? The look of the shop? The friendliness of the staff? And how do different clothes shops project different images to attract their target customers? A shop window with a small number of garments with "designer" labels, a few well-chosen props, lots of space and a plain background, projects an exclusive up-market image. In contrast, a window stuffed full of garments, the only props being there to support the wares and large price labels with the prices marked boldly in red would certainly project the "stack 'em high, sell 'em cheap" image!

What Image To Project?

So what image should you try to project? In essence you should be attempting to match your target customer's *expectations* and *needs*, ie to reflect what they are looking for.

Any image is in fact a mixture of elements which taken together make a unique blend. However one core element with almost every image is the "price point" the business is aiming at and this decision will have a marked

bearing on the more minor elements of the image mix.

Price Point There are basically three price point levels which have the characteristics shown in the box.

There is no simple recipe for success based on any philosophy such as "we aim at the top-end of the market as they've lots of money to spend" or "all our goods are cheap so everyone can afford them". Business, profitable business, can be made at any price point but, not surprisingly, the characteristics of a business aiming at the very top end will be completely different to another business aiming at the bottom. So it is important, even essential, to know which market you are aiming at.

Top-End
Exclusive; Prestigious; Up-market.
Products: Designer Label; Expensive brands.
Services: Supply blue-chip clients. Selective.
Customer base small but can afford the premium prices & less affected by recession.

Middle Market
Value For Money.
Products: Branded; Own-label.
Services: Very diversified.
Customer base large but many competing for same customers & vulnerable in recession.

Bottom End
Cheap; Discount, Mass Market.
Products: Unbranded.
Services: Limited to essentials.
Customer base large but spending power limited both in quantity and range of goods or services likely to be purchased.

Other Image Options As already mentioned, a unique image involves quite a mixture of elements. Some of these are listed below:

Cheapness This is not just the first,

Projecting The Right Image

alphabetically, but probably one of the most common images businesses try to project. Cheapness can be conveyed by a "cheap & nasty" image or a "super value cheap" image, an example of the latter being discount warehouses.

There are many ways to convey cheapness but they all stress *price*. The business name may also reflect this. Advertisements may stress factors which allow the price to be low, such as selling direct from the factory. Any premises or displays will have a "no frills", utility look.

Competence/Credibility Obviously this is highly relevant when you are selling expertise — either in terms of your products or services. Such expertise could embrace artistic, professional or technical areas of business. Manufacturers of high-tech products, designers, consultancies and business-to-business operations would all be suitable examples where their image should reflect competence.

This can be conveyed in a number of ways. If the Owners or Directors have suitable professional qualifications, they could be shown after their names whenever quoted on letterheads etc. Membership of relevant trade associations could also be mentioned. If a business has traded for several years, credibility can also be projected by stating how long it has been established.

If the business already has "blue-chip" client companies (such as local government or national companies with well-known household names) it may be possible to mention this fact as you can gain a great deal of credibility by this means — it might be tactful to obtain their permission first if planning to do this very overtly. Competence and credibility can also be reflected visually by photos of your premises (but only if they are impressive) and photos of staff doing the type of clever work you are trying to project.

Convenience This can be in terms of location (ie near to your potential customers); by trading for extended hours; by offering customers an "everything under one roof" service or by a convenient delivery/collection service.

Such convenience is often projected by the name of the venture or by the use of a prominent slogan, eg "24 hour Service" or "Open 8 Till Late". It also has to shout a bit so signs, advertisements etc need to be bold. There is little point in taking a low profile.

Customer Service Two words which are frequently mentioned but far less often seen in practice! Of course, every business must consider customer service as one of

The Evolution Of Jantzen's Diving Girl. How a famous swimwear manufacturer changed their logo over the years to keep it up to date by subtle changes which did not alter the original concept. (Reg'd Trade Mark: Jantzen Inc USA. Reproduced here with their kind permission)

their primary objectives, for no satisfied customers = no business!

In practice, you can consciously project a friendly, caring image. For instance, the signatory on all letters could use his or her first name and surname rather than simply an initial; advertisements and brochures might show pictures of contact people looking welcoming; the entrance and point of business area (be it office, shop or whatever) should look inviting (which applies also to factories which are too often very uninviting). These all help to project a positive image. Even the wording used in letters, adverts and leaflets can be made more friendly. In such literature you might also highlight aspects of your business service which are customer care orientated, for instance by nominating a member of staff as the Customer Contact person and making him/her readily available.

An important element of customer service is the telephone. Whilst the technique is important, ie what you say and how you say it, it is also vital that phones are answered speedily. Small firms without an office that is always manned should consider using a telephone answering machine as lost calls may be lost business.

The final (and most important part) is staff training so they realise the crucial nature of Customer Service.

Design/Fashion Here the description covers any business that survives by selling its design/creative expertise or sense of fashion (in the widest sense).

A dull, boring image would be a huge let down. Even more care is required. A problem with projecting a fashionable image is that it will reflect styles/designs in vogue which will naturally become obsolete in a relatively short time. This image will therefore require more frequent re-vamping than others.

Exclusivity Think of the image of a top-notch motor car. One of its attractions is that there will be few others like it on the road. Exclusivity may be the appropriate image if you are producing a small volume, high value product.

International Capability A small business trying to win overseas contracts or sales or perhaps trying to acquire an agency from an overseas company would obviously benefit from portraying this image.

Simply adding the words "United Kingdom" to your address block and a fax or telex number (where available) is a good start. If you are dealing with one specific country, a neat touch is to include the full phone dialling code from that country to the UK. Also if dealing with non-English speaking countries, a few words translated into their language is an effective way of indicating you really do mean business. If you have a contact/Agent/Rep abroad, you might print that on your stationery too.

Intimacy Some nightclubs, ladies hairdressing salons, beauticians, cocktail bars and clothes shops may choose to reflect this image.

Such intimacy can be created by subdued lighting, subtle decor, hushed sounds and a general feeling of closeness.

National Capability Despite the UK being a relatively small place, buyers can at times be strangely parochial. If you feel this may be the case, the ability to demonstrate a national capability is therefore most important.

The traditional way to indicate a national presence is by including that in your trading name. However, business names which include words such as "National, International, British, European, United Kingdom, Scotland, Scottish, England, English, Ireland, Irish, Wales, Welsh etc etc" require special permission. Get a copy of the booklet "Business Names And Business Ownership" from a Companies House (whose addresses are listed on page 22). Alternatively, your stationery might include a phrase such as "Offices in ..." which then lists several places around the country.

Prestige This can be an important image angle if you are trying to sell to large operations who like to think they are dealing with a well-established company. Or you may be dealing with wealthy clientele, or those that simply like to pretend they are wealthy!

Prestige can be conveyed by a suitable choice of trading name, address, carefully chosen style of letterhead, brochure and, finally, decor (if clients need to visit you).

Quality This is another word which is much quoted, less frequently achieved, but should be an essential ingredient of most business images.

It can be projected in a number of ways depending upon the business sector in which you are trading. Manufacturers may stress quality in terms of dedicated quality control staff and procedures they use, and compliance with the appropriate British Standard. Service orientated businesses may reflect this in terms of well-known (and dependable) brand names they use or sell or quality conscious (business) customers they deal with.

Projecting The Right Image

Even the quality of a letterhead and brochure can reflect the thought given to overall quality in any company. In fact a general attention to detail is an essential part of a quality image.

Comments from satisfied customers (who are identified, not simply as "Ms A.B. of London") can also help.

Simply stating that you are concerned with quality does not impress buyers much these days.

Rapid Response This is where a business projects that it can provide a rapid response to a customer's requirements, for instance a quick car tyre & exhaust fitting centre, an instant print business or an emergency plumbing/electrical repairs service.

Such an image is very often reflected in the name of the business and all their advertising reflects the quick, instant, rapid work they can do.

It is also vital to make phone and fax numbers obvious in any communication, brochure or advertisement. You could also highlight it in the Phone Book and Yellow Pages.

Reliability There are two types of reliability — the reliability associated with machinery and the reliability of a company in terms of it doing what it claims it will do.

Some of the ways of trying to project this image are similar to the comments under **Quality** above, with the added point that reliability, by its very nature, needs to be proven over time. However, after suitable time has elapsed there is mileage in stating that you have achieved certain reliability targets. Excellent guarantees (which actually work when put to the test) can also provide customer confidence.

Size To some customers, the size of organisation they are dealing with is important. This can be conveyed on a letterhead by, for instance, listing the number of retail outlets you have or listing the number of partners or Directors in the firm. Promotional literature could mention the size of workforce, annual turnover or the production capacity.

This list is not intended to be exhaustive, rather to give some of the more popular image ingredients and how they might be projected.

What's In A Name?

For a small business, particularly one that is relatively new, a key way to project a sharp image is to chose a trading name that reflects exactly that desired image. It is a simple, yet very successful strategy — as shown by Kwik-Fit, Country Casuals and Kall-Kwik Printing to mention just a few.

A tricky situation can occur where a name which was ideal at one time becomes less so with the passage of time. This affects businesses of all sizes and the usual remedy is to change the name in stages so people have time to get used to the new one.

Logos, Brand Names & Slogans

Logos A logo is a unique symbol (or "device" as it is called) by which you hope customers will identify you and your product or service. We are all familiar with logos and it can be an important promotional tool, saving space when having to print anything. It should, by clever design, also say something about your business. However, it does usually take a long time (and in the case of the consumer market, a large promotional budget) before people recognise them. Further-

more the design of a good logo usually requires a professional graphics designer, as an amateur design looks just that. But once a logo has been produced the artwork can be reused many times on brochures, advertisements, packaging etc.

Brand Names A brand name is the name on a label or packaging by which it is recognised. It is not always the same as the company's name. For instance the Marks and Spencer's brand name is "St Michael". If a company's products are diversified, it may not be possible for it to have a trading name that covers its different products, and the use of different brand names may help its marketing. As with logos, where the customer base is relatively small (eg if you are dealing with only a couple of hundred businesses) then they will soon get to know any logo and/or brand name you use. In that situation they can therefore be useful tools. However, when you are dealing with a consumer market of many thousand customers the chances are they will not recognise your logo or brand name for quite some time unless you have a very substantial promotional (ie advertising or PR) budget.

Sales Slogans A Sales Slogan is a catchy message which can be used in advertising, on letterheads, leaflets, invoices, on radio commercials and so on. They are not just simply a sales tool as they usually reflect the unique selling proposition of the business and this has an important bearing on the image the company tries to project about itself.

Packaging

The design and manufacture of packaging for products has become a very sophisticated industry in itself.

A GOOD EXAMPLE OF A CO-ORDINATED CORPORATE IMAGE

Kall Kwik
PRINT COPY DESIGN

711 Great Western Road
Glasgow
G12 8QX

Telephone 041-334 9272
Fax 041-334 7170

Alan Cochrane
Proprietor

Kall Kwik
PRINT COPY DESIGN

711 Great Western Road
Glasgow
G12 8QX

Telephone 041-334 9272
Fax 041-334 7170

MEMO

711 Great Western Road
Glasgow G12 8QX

Telephone: 041-334 9272
Fax: 041-334 7170

Kall Kwik
PRINT COPY DESIGN

Postcode

Telephone No

Customer Ref

Kall Kwik
PRINT COPY DESIGN

711 Great Western Road, Glasgow G12 8QX. Telephone: 041-334 9272 F

CATEGORY	QUANTITY	DESCRIPTION
1 Printing		
2 Origination		
3 Supplies		
4 Photocopying		
5 Other Sales		
6 Finishing		
7		
8		

Goods Rec
Terms - Cas
N.B. A charge
TO RE-ORDER

ease tear off

1 Great

With compliments

Kall-Kwik's corporate identity in red and blue gives a strong, consistent appearance to the quick-print franchise's national network. All of Kall-Kwik Printing's promotional material, stationery, shop signs, packaging and even corporate clothing is designed to feature their corporate identity. Every aspect plays a part in reinforcing the Kall-Kwik marque in customers' minds, strengthening market awareness of Kall-Kwik and greatly enhancing the impact of any promotional activity.

Kall Kwik
PRINT COPY DESIGN

711 Great Western Road
Glasgow
G12 8QX

Telephone 041-334 9272
Fax 041-334 7170

Projecting The Right Image

Packaging not only has to be attractive to a would-be buyer, but it also has to compete with other products, perhaps on the same shelf. Although you might first think of packaging in terms of consumer products, good and attractive packaging is now very important for trade purchases — even the humble spanner is likely to come in a presentation bubble pack.

In addition to making the packaging visually attractive, today's packaging designer has also to consider:

Storage & Transit The packaging needs to protect the contents whilst in storage and during transit. Its physical dimensions and shape have to allow it to fit inside any external cardboard container that may be needed to ship the goods in bulk.

Display By use of clear windows, cut-outs, rigid bubble or other means, the packaging has to reveal the attractive features of the contents. Using glass jars for jams is a simple example of this. In many retail situations the size and shape of the packaging is important so that it will fit display shelving and allow the retailer a dense concentration of goods. Some products require hanging for which the packaging also has to allow. Many products now require bar coding too. A supplier of bar codes is Kings Town Photocodes Ltd, Waltham House, River-view Road, Beverley, Yorkshire HU17 8DY. Tel: 0482-867321.

Attention Catcher It has been estimated that the average supermarket shopper scans four feet of shelving from top to bottom in one second! From a crowded shelf the packaging of your product has to stand out as the most attractive and let the would-be buyer know what its contents are without any ambiguity.

Corporate Identity The packaging must also reflect the corporate identity of the company, establishing the same "look" as any other products the company produces.

Legalities In certain trade sectors, eg food, the labelling has also to contain important legally required information. Contact your local Trading Standards Officer for more information.

Play The "Green" Card Waste generated by packaging is a major ecological problem. Increasingly manufacturers will need to respond to pressures from conscientious buyers for more bio-degradable and re-usable packaging.

Price Packaging can amount to a hefty part of the cost of an item. Be sure to research the options and their costs fully. Try to think laterally and maybe come up with something original or quite simply *better* than other comparable products on the market. For instance, someone was first to put shampoo in small satchets and someone else thought of selling large calendars complete with convenient envelopes ready for posting. Packaging can often be a very cost effective way to improve an image. Whilst there are obviously design and origination costs, these are one-off and the end result can last for years. Good packaging sells!

Image Is Everything — Everything Is Image

Every external manifestation of a business projects an image of that company — the letterhead (and how letters are written), business cards, brochures, order forms, advertisements, the address, business name, logo, brand name(s), sales slogans, packaging, premises, exterior signs, interior decor, the company's vehicles, staff clothing, even the size and style of cheque book used and so on. These are all tangible factors, but the less tangible aspects such as how a Receptionist greets visitors, how the telephone is answered and how sales staff handle customers are equally important.

To make the most of your image projection, it is obviously sensible to co-ordinate all the aspects listed above to enable colours and themes to run through everything. Your staff should fully understand what image they are supposed to project. The phrase for this is "corporate image" and it makes sense even on a small scale.

Consistency is an important point. The achievement of a distinctive image is not an overnight job. If the approach is one of chop and change, then the only image projected will be one of confusion.

However, an exciting discovery about "image" is that done correctly, a small business can project a super image with little extra expense, just by some thought and effort.

P.S. In this Chapter we have considered the image of a business and its products or service as being the same. However you can have the situation where a business has products or services each of which projects a different image appropriate to their target markets ■

Planning The "Market Entry"

Introduction

When considering the launch of a new business, project or product you need to consider just how you are going to enter the market. This "Market Entry" as it is called, can be achieved in several different ways. For instance, you might do a joint venture with another company that is already operating in that market or you might even consider buying out another small company that is in that market. Whatever strategy you chose requires some planning, just like any other aspect of Marketing.

Fit And Ready?

Even assuming thorough market research indicates that there is indeed a market opportunity, a question to consider is simply — is the project actually fit and ready to be launched? It sounds obvious but we all tend to be optimists and in our enthusiasm to see our projects become a reality, timescales are usually rushed. The possibility of problems arising are either ignored or given scant attention. There is usually little provision made for contingencies.

Surprisingly few projects at the moment of launch are fully organised with all staff trained and the necessary back-up (documentation, procedures, spares, stock or whatever) in place. What usually happens is that there is a heroic and desperate corner-cutting struggle to launch the new venture on time. Not only is this very wearing on all concerned but the project is now highly vulnerable.

This vulnerability can stem from a competitor's counter-attack, customer disappointment or simply low sales because of insufficient stock, inadequate staff training etc.

To avoid or at least reduce this requires planning.

Timing

One of the most important matters to consider when doing any planning is the *timing*.

Most small businesses simply launch their new business or project as soon as they can, even if this is singularly not the best time. For instance, specialist shops that open in January or February miss the important Christmas season. Manufacturers whose new products are launched too late to appear at a major trade show miss the opportunity of letting trade buyers see the goods, and so on. The urge to launch as soon as you can, even if the timing is poor, is often overwhelming, with the desire to generate cashflow and get in front of competitors, but if the timing is not good the whole project may be jeopardised.

In terms of Market Entry, the timing aspects to consider include seasonal changes (ie when is the *customer* ready to buy rather than *you* ready to supply) and the actual or likely activity of the competition.

While still on the subject of timing, where a product is concerned, other aspects to consider include the lead time of producing and fully testing the new product (new products never oblige by keeping on schedule!), and producing adequate stock to meet demand. For a service business, staff training can be critical too. Where new premises are involved, again much time can be spent finding suitable premises and then negotiating lease or purchase details.

Project Launch

The launch of a new project, product or service is a major marketing opportunity which should not be missed. What is the objective? Simply, to gain the maximum publicity (this is referred to as "exposure") for the new venture so that your potential customers are made aware of it as quickly as possible.

Getting this publicity requires some orchestration of the event, the precise details of which depends on just who is launching what, but the concepts are basically the same.

Publicity is achieved by:

1. Use of the media through editorial.
2. Use of the media through bought advertising.
3. Inviting potential customers to see what you are offering.

"I have great pleasure in launching this new range of prestigious conservatories....."

Planning The "Market Entry"

These aspects of promotion are covered in great detail in the following Section of this book, however some points relevant to a Project Launch "ceremony" should be mentioned here.

The Launch Ceremony

To attract both media attention and buyers, you can stage an "event". Great ingenuity has been demonstrated in recent years by companies putting on the most bizarre or dramatic events to ensure they attract attention. However you can stage a much more modest event and still gain suitable exposure.

Typically the event which a small business might organise will include some VIP performing an opening ceremony with invitations going to local Press and potential customers. Whereas public figures, Mayors and other civic dignitaries usually make no charge for appearing, TV or Radio personalities usually do make a charge (the better known ones can command several thousand pounds for a brief appearance). The only justification for using any VIP is to increase the likelihood of the media using the story and (where appropriate) for potential customers to come to the event. Any costs likely to be incurred therefore have to be seen in this light.

The ceremony will also usually include some refreshments and an opportunity for the business to show off its latest venture, possibly with some sort of demonstration. While a static display can make a useful background, people are more likely to respond to some active demonstration or video.

For a manufacturing concern the launch ceremony could take place at the factory but if this is out of the way or not salubrious enough then a Hotel could be used as a suitable venue. A retail business would normally have the ceremony at the shop premises while an office-based business may chose its office or a Hotel. Again, some ingenuity may lead to an alternative, more unusual, location being chosen.

Details which need to be considered include — ensuring there is someone to welcome the guests; providing name badges for staff (and possibly guests); Press Packs for any journalists present and some promotional literature for the other guests to take away with them; lots for people to see; waiter/waitress service for drinks and light refreshments and possibly the opportunity of giving a Presentation (see Chapter **Promoting Sales)**■

ADVERTISING, PROMOTION & SALES

Chapters

Advertising, Promotion & Sales

Introduction

This Section looks at ways of finding new customers and selling more to existing ones. When you produce a new product, open a new shop, set up a new service ... you might ask yourself at the moment of launch "How many likely customers know about this?". The project might be at the centre of your own world but may be completely unknown to anyone else! You can have a good product or service to offer at a good price but if too few potential customers know about it, the business will fail. Equally, if your sales techniques are poor the business will also suffer.

Sometimes one hears comments like "We don't need to do any promotion, we've got all the work we can handle" or maybe "Everyone knows we are the best suppliers of..." or perhaps "Our competitors don't do any advertising so why should we?"

These are all examples of potentially complacent thinking. But if you are still doubtful about the need to spend time and money on promoting your business, then think of it another way — if you embark, fully committed, on a promotional campaign, even if it does not result in the hoped-for additional sales, it may either:

a) Indicate that there is in fact a limited market for whatever product or service you are offering, and/or
b) Provide valuable feed-back from customers which will indicate in which direction the business should head.

Every successful sale requires four steps to be taken. These are:

> **Seek** out customers
> **Stimulate** their interest
> **Satisfy** their needs
> **Sell!**

Although in practice the four steps may not be so distinct, each step has still to be taken. When planning your sales strategy it is useful to bear this in mind for if any of the four steps are weak or missing the chances of a successful sale will be reduced or be non-existent.

There are many ways of finding customers and even a small business should use a combination of these. Some ways are more costly than others while some are more effective. Unfortunately (or perhaps, fortunately) cost and effect are not always clearly related! The different promotional methods are basically:

1. Advertising
2. Issuing Leaflets & Brochures
3. Getting articles in the Media
4. Taking a Stand at an Exhibition
5. Doing Special Promotions

These are all covered fully in the Chapters that follow. The specialised method of Direct Mail was covered in the earlier Chapter **Sorting Out The Sales Distribution**. In addition there is a Chapter later in this section of the book devoted entirely to **Selling Techniques**.

Advertising is sometimes referred to as "above the line promotion" while producing leaflets and taking a Stand at Exhibitions is called "below the line promotion".

Unique Selling Proposition

Your business will have a better chance of succeeding if it offers a "unique selling proposition", ie a product or service that customers cannot obtain elsewhere. This does not necessarily require the whole business to be unique but there must be something different about what you offer or the way you offer it. This could be the style or features of your service, your packaging, detail features of your product, your "own label" goods, price, originality of display etc. Whatever this uniqueness is should be stressed in any advertisement, leaflet, mailshot, Press Release or other promotion.

The Promotional Budget

It may seem a difficult task to work out how much to budget for promotion and frankly, it is! The more so for a new or recently established business with little or no trading record. However, sensible decisions have to be made and here we suggest an approach which should give a guide as to how much you need to spend. Doubtless as your plan unfolds, experience will cause you to make modifications to your original plans and budget.

The amount of money you need to allocate to promotion depends on a number of factors such as how new your business or product is, where your premises are located, the type of customers you are aiming at and so on. Obviously, if your workshop is down a back lane, few people will know you are there so you need to spend some money letting people know what your business does and where you are to be found. More money will need to be spent if your business is new.

A common way of expressing promotional budgets is in terms of a percentage of forecast turnover, ie a budget of 3% on a forecast business turnover of £100,000 would mean you expect to spend £3,000 on promotion (excluding direct costs of salespeople).

Method   In this method we start with a typical average promotional figure of 3% and then modify that "median"

Advertising, Promotion & Sales

TABLE FOR ESTIMATING THE PROMOTIONAL BUDGET			
FACTOR	SUBTRACT 1%	MEDIAN (3%)	ADD 1%
Age of Business	Established	Young	New
Age of Product	Established	Young	New
Degree of Innovation	Nothing Unusual	Some innovative details	Very innovative Clients need educn.
Premises Location	Prime. Hi-profile Nr Customers	Not quite prime	Remote. Low-profile Not seen by clients
Customers	Trade	—	Consumer
Agent/Distributor Network	Good Coverage	Limited	None
Competition	None	Benign	Hostile
Special Factors	Yes — less need to promote	None	Yes — more need to promote

figure depending on the particular circumstances facing your business. This is shown in the table above and then two examples below illustrate how the method is put into practice.

From experience we have chosen a figure of 3% as a typical average promotional figure, which we call the median in the table. This is simply a ball-park figure to start from.

Note that some of the factors in the table will not be relevant to your type of business in which case they should simply be ignored.

Example Consider a new specialist shop, open only a few months, and located in a good town centre site (but not a prime High Street location). To calculate a promotional budget, we start with the median figure of 3%, then the calculation would be:
Age...add 1%;
Premises Location...median;
Customers...add 1%.
The other factors are either the median or not relevant so the promotional budget for this business should be:
3% + 1% + 1% = 5%.

Example For a completely different example, let us consider a small electronics firm, several years old, in an out-of-the-way location and about to launch a new energy saving product for hotels. The company has a number of distributors and there is no direct competitor. Its calculation would be:
Age...median;
Age of Product...add 1%;
Degree of Innovation...add 1%;
Premises Location...add 1%;
Customers...subtract 1%;
Distribution...subtract 1% and
Competition...subtract 1%.
The estimated promotional budget would then work out as the median,
3% + 1% + 1% + 1% − 1% − 1% − 1% = 3%

It must be emphasised that this method is not "set in stone" so should be interpreted in the light of your own circumstances.

There is, however, a way to do a quick check on the figure you calculate. Consider the different promotional activities outlined in the following Chapters, make a list of those you feel necessary to achieve your sales targets with an indication of likely costs, then add up all these figures and compare that with your calculated budget.

Joint Promotions Your budget for promotion can be increased with some co-operation from other interested parties. For instance, a retailer may get support from a supplier paying up to half the cost of an ad if his product is the only one shown, his brand name and/or logo is clearly seen and, usually, he has vetted the ad before printing. Other examples of co-operation could be a fabric supplier may pay part of a garment manufacturer's ad or a printer, graphics studio and book-binder may produce a joint leaflet.

Don't Forget Your Customers
It is perhaps too easy to forget that the quickest, easiest way to expand sales is to try to SELL MORE TO EXISTING CUSTOMERS rather than simply looking around for new ones.

Invest In Promotion
And finally, all promotional activity should be seen as an investment not just a cost burden or something tagged on at the end. Promotion should not be done just when "there's some spare cash", and shunned when business is booming "so no need to" or when business is slack "can't afford it!"

But just as an investment must show a return so must your promotions produce results. There is no point putting even small sums of money into one particular line of your campaign when it shows no tangible results. Start by doing a test run and if that does not work, try something else until you find what works for your own business ■

Advertising — Why? Where? When?

Introduction

When people consider "promotion" they tend to think first of advertising, but advertising is only one part of the promotional mix.

Many small businesses have had unhappy experiences with advertising. Perhaps they spent a lot of money and saw little response in terms of increased sales. They might also have been the victims of unscrupulous advertising salespeople who were more concerned with the commission they earned than the proper development of the client's business. These experiences may have discouraged the small business from further advertising and possibly other promotions too.

Five of the biggest misconceptions about advertising are: a) confusing "promotion" with "advertising"; b) not advertising in case you will be unable to cope with the expected rush (few businesses, except for some Direct Mail companies, are in this privileged position and many overestimate the likely response speed to any advertising); c) thinking that advertising is always a waste of money as past experiences have been unsuccessful; d) assuming that for an ad to be successful requires it to be an expensive full colour page in a glossy publication and e) thinking that "to advertise" means placing a solitary ad every so often. For an advertising campaign to be successful it normally requires a planned series of advertisements which are a part of an integrated marketing plan.

Advertising can and does work in the *right* context. What makes it work sometimes for some people and fail sometimes for others?

A lack of success with advertising can be for a number of reasons, such as: a) there is little market interest in what is on offer; b) there is a lack of expertise in putting together a successful ad and advertising campaign or c) the advertising is not targeted closely enough.

Far too many small businesses, once they either make the decision (or are co-erced into making the decision) to place an advertisement, then pay scant attention to what the ad needs to say, how it will be designed, where in the publication it is likely to appear, and so on. It is therefore hardly surprising that the results are sometimes very disappointing.

Successful Advertising

There are 6 main elements to a successful advertising campaign. These are:

1. Ensuring (by proper Market Research) that there is a genuine *need* for what you plan to advertise.
2. Defining clearly the objectives of the advertising, ie *why* you advertise.
3. Using the correct media, ie *where* you place the advertisements.
4. Timing when the advertisements appear, ie *when* you advertise.
5. Designing the advertisement, ie *how* you advertise.
6. Monitoring the results and changing accordingly, ie learning *which* advertisements are the most effective.

The first point above merits further comment for no ad will succeed if the market is not interested in what is on offer. This also relates to timing as a response to a new ad campaign is only likely if the prospective customer ("prospect") has a *need* at precisely the time of seeing or hearing the ad. It is for just that reason that small firms offering domestic services such as joinery, plumbing, roof repairs etc need to do almost continuous advertising.

In any trade sector, with regular advertising, an on-going awareness can be built up which may influence a later buying decision.

This Chapter (which looks at the *why, where* and *when* to advertise) and the next Chapter (which looks at *how* to produce the ad and monitor the results) will hopefully provide the basic information needed to advertise successfully.

WHY ADVERTISE

Often an advertisement is placed because of some vague notion that it might help sales. You need to be much more precise than that. Although the long-term idea is to increase sales the immediate objective of an advertisement can be different. For instance, consider the options in the box below:

Situation: New Product
Objectives: To increase Buyer awareness; to back up exposure at an Exhibition or to assist Reps on the road.

Situation: Existing Product
Objectives: To increase sales by attracting people to visit you, to assist Reps or to encourage direct response.

Situation: Direct Mail
Objective: To achieve a sales response.

Situation: Address Change
Objective: To let customers know how to find you.

Situation: Exhibition/Special Event
Objective: To encourage people to visit your Stand or Special Event.

Situation: Staff
Objective: To recruit new staff/Agents.

Advertising — Why? Where? When?

Clearly different types of advertisement are needed for these different situations.

A key advantage of advertising over certain other forms of promotion, eg sending out Press Releases, is that you can *control* what is being said and where and when it is being said. This can be very important indeed.

Some small businesses may have in fact no need to advertise at all, relying instead on other promotional means to achieve their objectives.

WHERE TO ADVERTISE

The choice of where to advertise is seemingly unlimited but for any specific business the number of *effective* places is much more restricted. The box below gives a general overview of the most popular media.

Some less common media which may be suitable for certain small businesses include "transport advertising", where you use the sides of buses or taxis, the posters on the escalators of tube stations or inside the tube trains themselves. You can also advertise on the tiny space available on parking meters or the very large space afforded by a cinema screen. Another medium is the hoardings around the edge of a football pitch, which is especially attractive when matches are regularly televised from those grounds.

The best media are those whose readership or audience most closely relates to your target market and its buying habits. That statement may seem fairly simple but it embraces two fundamental concepts.

Although it is important that the medium matches your market it must also reflect how buyers go about making their purchasing decisions. Thus certain Trade or Association Directories though they might match your market may not match buyers

Advertising Method	Cost	Good Points	Bad Points
Direct mailshot letter	Low	Targeted audience. High response rate (2% to 5% or perhaps more).	Time consuming to carry out, partly as it takes time to locate or produce a good mailing list.
Small Poster	Low	Large readership. Long life.	Limited to where posters are allowed. Message must be short.
Letterbox leaflet	Low	Can be part-targeted. Low response rate (usually well under 1%).	Difficult to distribute effectively unless done by eg Post Office, which increases the cost.
Directories (eg Yellow Pages)	Low/Med	Advert life is 1yr. Allows comparison with competitors.	Can only make changes annually and ensure you use a relevant Directory.
Direct mailshot leaflet	Low/Med	Targeted audience. Response rate highly variable.	Time consuming to carry out (but less time than personalised direct mailshot letter).
Advert in local newspaper	Med	Local audience. Can repeat often. Usually some supporting editorial is possible.	Readership much larger than your target. Advert has to compete for reader's attention. Today's news, tomorrow's fish & chip paper!
Advert in trade publication	Med/High	Targeted. Editorial may be possible. Long life. Often a Reader Enquiry Service.	If publication relevant, none, except price.
Advert on Local Radio	Med/High	Wide audience. Suits certain consumer and business markets.	Advert life very brief so needs repeating frequently.
Advert in national newspaper or magazine	High	National audience. Can repeat often. Colour usually available on some pages.	As per local paper and editorial mention less likely. Ensure likely sales will cover costs.
Advert in "glossy" magazine	High	Some targeting possible. Full colour available on most pages.	Need to book space months ahead. High cost of advert production.

habits (ie they do not actually refer to the Directory when wanting to buy something) so an advertisement would be a waste of money. Similarly, "special features" which are much loved by newspapers to drum up advertising from selected trade sectors do not necessarily match buyers habits. Since these features can be the subject of hard selling, this cautionary note is worth heeding.

Also, although it may be good for the ego to see your full colour advert in one of the national glossy consumer colour magazines (which, incidentally can cost you anything up to £25,000 plus the photography and other charges) it would be a remarkable waste of money if your business had only one retail outlet and no mail order facilities or other means of national distribution.

Simply following blindly what your competitors are doing is not necessarily correct either, though equally if no competitor is using the same medium then you should ask yourself why.

If you are still a little overawed with the potential choice, perhaps the table (top right) may help.

To find out the names of publications, their addresses and details of their advertising charges, you need to consult a copy of BRAD.

BRAD This is a monthly publication which lists every newspaper, business journal, consumer publication, independent TV and commercial radio station in the UK, together with other vital information needed by any would-be advertiser. BRAD is available on subscription (currently £385) from BRAD, Maclean Hunter House, Chalk Lane, Cockfosters Road, Barnet EN4 0BU, tel: 081-441 6644 or a copy may

CUSTOMER TYPE	CUSTOMER DISTRIBUTION	ADVERTISING OPTIONS (For typical small business)
Consumer	Local	Local newspaper(s)/Radio; Letterbox leaflet; Local mags; Yellow Pages; Posters; Buses
Consumer	National/Regional	National or regional newspaper(s); National Consumer magazines
Trade	Local	Yellow Pages; Special feature in local newspaper(s); Direct mailshot
Trade	National/Regional	Trade publications; Direct mailshot; Trade Directories

Note: The table does not apply to Exporters

be seen at most main public libraries. A typical entry taken from BRAD is reproduced below.

CAR
Affiliations ABC PPA
EMAP National Publications Ltd, 97 Earls Court Road, London W8 6QH. 071-370 0333. Fax 071-373 7544. Monthly — second Thurs of month preceding cover date. Copy — mono 4 weeks; 4 colour 5 weeks. Cancellation — mono 9 weeks; colour 19 weeks preceding copy date. Single copy £2.20. Per year £29.40. Agency Commission 10%
Rate card effective January 1991 (excl. VAT)

Standard Rates

	1	6	12
page	£2,642.00	£2,571.00	£2,379.00
half	£1,394.00	£1,323.00	£1,255.00
quarter	£726.00	£690.00	£653.00
eighth	£365.00	£347.00	£329.00

Cover Rates £6,455
Colour Rates 4 colour, page £5,937. Series 6 — £5,640 12 — £5,343. Two colour, page £3,847. Series 6 — £3,654 12 — £3,462.
Bleed Pages 10% extra
Special Positions Facing matter 10% extra
Inserts Accepted by arrangement
Mechanical Data Type page size 271 x 194, half 271 x 95 or 130 x 194, quarter 130 x 95 or 64 x 194, eighth 64 x 95. Bleed pages 297 x 219. Trim size 291 x 216. Web-offset litho
Executives Editor, Gavin Green. Group Advertisement Manager, Hilary Field. Advertisement Manager, Helen Morkel
Circulation (Jan-June 1991) ABC 137,105

	Total	UK	Overseas
N'Trade (Pd Full)	130,245	107,675	22,570
Subs (Pd Full)	6,403	3,090	3,313
O/Unpd	457	403	54

Reproduced from BRAD
with kind permission

Media Pack Once you have identified a number of interesting publications, the next step is to phone their advertising departments and ask for a "Media Pack". It is also useful to ask for their "advance features list" which will give you details of special feature articles (or programmes) that they are planning, one of which may be exactly appropriate to your particular business.

The Media Pack normally consists of a copy of the publication, a Rate Card and details of their "circulation". The Rate Card gives all the advertising costs, which are called "rates", (as you will have seen in BRAD), technical data and their trading terms.

The Media Pack should also include the all-important "copy date" for each issue. This is the deadline by which all advertising material must be received. Ignore it at your peril!

For display adverts (ie those adverts in their own box), these costs are usually expressed in terms of a full page, half page, quarter page and sometimes eighth and sixteenth page sizes. Or they may be quoted in terms of the cost per single column centimetre (scc). This latter measurement

Advertising – Why? Where? When?

is a space one column wide and one centimetre deep – obviously you need a number of centimetres for an advert, and there may be a minimum size.

Where a publication is only printed partly in colour, the rates may be quoted as "mono" (ie black and white) with colour charged extra.

Classified ads in contrast are usually expressed in terms of cost per word or cost per line (called "lineage"). Sometimes you can have a display advertisement in the classified section in which case it will usually be quoted in terms of cost per scc.

Circulation The "circulation" of a publication is the number of copies it sells or distributes. You also need to know who these readers are. This is obviously important for if the readers are not the same as your target market, then you will be wasting your money. To put this another way, if only ⅓rd of a publication's readers are likely customers, it means that ⅔rds of your ad cost is a complete waste of cash! Most publications have their circulations verified independently – by ABC (Audit Bureau of Circulations) for paid-for and controlled-circulation publications and BVS (Bulk Verification Services) or VFD (Verified Free Distribution) for free consumer publications. This data is given in BRAD, but the Media Pack may give more details, in particular a breakdown as to just who is reading the publication, and the more information you have the better. If the information provided does not answer all your questions, phone and ask the publication for more details.

"Readership", in contrast to "circulation" is the estimated number of people who see each issue, so is likely to be several times that figure given for the "circulation".

Many trade publications have what is called a "Controlled Circulation". This means copies are sent out free (the magazine is supported by the advertising it carries) but circulation is restricted to those in the trade, possibly above a certain managerial level.

A criticism levelled against both trade and consumer publications which are issued free is that since people do not have to pay for them (and particularly with consumer free publications, may not even wish to see them), their circulation figures cannot be compared directly with figures for paid-for publications. It is argued that someone who pays for a publication is more likely to read it than someone who has received one free. This is probably more true for those general consumer publications which have little or no editorial.

Local Newspapers/Radio If you plan to advertise in a local newspaper or on local radio, it is worth taking the trouble to visit and speak to the Advertising Manager. He or she will also be able to advise which day(s) are best for the advertisement(s) and in which part of the paper (or for radio, which times of the day). They may also introduce you to one of their reporters. See also the Chapter **Working With The Media-PR.**

WHEN TO ADVERTISE

Many small businesses advertise when *they* are ready rather than timing the advertisement to when the *customer* is likely to be ready to buy.

In most businesses even if trading activity goes on throughout the year there are better times for selling when prospects are more likely to become customers. Advertising during off-peak or out-of-Season times may be cheaper but will often bring disappointing results.

A problem when launching a new product or service, opening new premises or whatever is this may not necessarily coincide with when potential buyers are in a buying mood. A further problem is that the media you choose have their own timescales which can be fairly inflexible. In many cases they require notification weeks in advance. Of course, compromises are usually possible but any advertising campaign does need to be planned.

A Series Of Ads Note the need to plan a "campaign", not simply plan an "advertisement" for rarely will one solitary ad, however brilliantly executed, achieve a satisfactory response. Placing a single ad is an error frequently made by inexperienced advertisers in the belief that almost "everyone" who sees the publication or hears the radio commercial will take it in and act on it. One natural objection to the idea of having a series of ads is the cost, but in that case it would still be better to plan three or four smaller ads than spend all your budget on one big advertisement.

Most advertising media offer "series discounts" which should be taken advantage of, though with a publication you have not used before it might be worthwhile trying a few ads first to see what response you get before committing yourself to a series.

Exposure Assuming that the correct medium is being used, the likelihood of an advertisement being seen depends on: a) the design of the advertisement; b) the position of the advertisement;

c) the size of the advertisement; d) the use of colour (in relation to competing ads/articles); e) the period of time the customer has an opportunity to see the advertisement and f) how often an advertisement is repeated.

Reinforcement The first time a potential customer sees or hears mention of a new business/product or service, the fact will very often be ignored or soon forgotten, unless the advertisement has some immediate relevance and impact. If he or she sees or hears another mention soon afterwards then there will, hopefully, be reinforcement and growing awareness.

This process of reinforcement continues each time the person is exposed to a mention of the new business/product or service (provided there is a theme running through so that they will be linked in the person's mind). This reinforcing combination can be achieved in several ways — editorial articles backing up advertising; recurring advertisements in the same publication; advertisements in different media that the same person might see or hear; an advertisement backing up a leaflet/brochure which the person has received; an advertisement reflecting a shop window theme; an advertisement backing up an appearance at an Exhibition, and so on.

This approach of backing up one line of promotion by another is usually the most effective one to adopt.

Timing To assist in planning, a simple calendar planner or flow chart as sketched (right) may help you with the inevitable juggling one has to do.

In this simple example, a manufacturer is launching a new product and the plan shows the first two advertisements placed in a monthly magazine. The advertisement is inviting the reader to send for a leaflet so that has to be produced on time also.

The same plan could also show Press Releases being sent out, Product timescales, Launch Ceremony details and so on ∎

	APRIL	MAY	JUNE	JULY
PRODUCT	▼ MOCK-UP READY TO PHOTO. ▼ CHECK PHOTOS		▼ INITIAL PRODUCTN RUN START	
LEAFLET	▼ SEE PRINTER ▼ DRAFT LEAFLET	▼ LEAFLET TO PRINTER ▼ CHECK PROOF ▼ COLLECT LEAFLETS		
MAGAZINE ADVERT	▼ BOOK ADVERT	▼ MAG. DEADLINE ▼ CHECK PROOF	▼ MAG. OUT ▼ NEXT ISSUE DEADLINE (SAME AD AS JUNE)	▼ MAG. OUT

SIMPLE PLANNER TO HELP ENSURE EVERYTHING HAPPENS ON TIME

Advertising — How?

The previous Chapter looked at *where* and *when* you should advertise. This Chapter discusses what to say in an ad and most importantly how to monitor the effectiveness of your advertising.

Image or Response Advertising?

In the context of this book, ads can be broadly categorised as "Image" or "Response" type advertisements.

Image Advertising This is where a company tries to link its product or service with a particular lifestyle or some other image aspect (see also the Chapter **Projecting The Right Image**). For instance a car maker may show a certain car model being suitably adored by the type of customer at whom they are aiming. The car will be photographed in a context appropriate to that person (or his aspirations), eg an off-road vehicle may be shown with the "hunting-shooting" set, a GT saloon car may be shown competing with sports cars on a race circuit and so on. This type of advertising is to help the company position its product or service in the appropriate part of the market place. It is therefore concerned with increasing (or reinforcing) the potential buyer's awareness of its brand or company name and the image the company wishes the buyer to link with that name. Thus the actual ads may vary but the strong image linking *theme* will remain constant.

Another key aspect of image advertising is that it rarely requests any direct response or action from the reader, listener or viewer though sometimes an address or phone number is tucked away somewhere, usually in small print. Such advertising tends to be the preserve of major companies who are selling cars, airline

travel, food, cosmetics, computers, confectionery, drink, consumer electronics etc and they are all mainly to do with image.

Response Advertising This is subtly different. Its main objective is to get a response from the person seeing or hearing the ad and if it does not produce this desired response then it has failed. Although 'image' can still be projected in a response ad, and may even be required in part to achieve the desired response, it is always a secondary aspect. For instance, whereas a car maker may run an image campaign at a national or regional level, the local car dealer who has to actually sell the cars, will tend to use response type ads.

Few small businesses can indulge in image advertising because the required advertising "spend" (ie budget) is relatively large and the effectiveness can only be judged many months or even years later in terms of percentage changes in sales, market share or by specially done market research. It is therefore response ads that we focus our attention on in this Chapter.

Since much of the advertising that we are exposed to, in glossy magazines and on TV, is of the image sort, many small businesses unwittingly mimic this in their own ads. They therefore produce an image ad when they in fact needed a response-type ad.

DESIGNING A DISPLAY AD

There are 5 parts to any good ad:
1. The Headline
2. Visuals (ie the illustrations)
3. Body Copy (ie the words)
4. Call for Action
5. Name & Address (& maybe Logo)

THE HEADLINE

This is the first hurdle and where many beginners stumble. To them their business and its name is understandably the most important thing in the whole world so they put their business name as the headline in big, bold letters. Unfortunately no-one else in the world really cares one bit about their business. The most important thing in the reader's life is *themselves* and what *they* want!

An exception where you might use the business name as the headline is if it is very descriptive as to what is on offer.

Normally the headline should be like a newspaper's front page headline — eye-catching! It should be punchy but not so short that there is no message, eg a company selling burglar alarms might have a headline BURGLAR ALARMS FOR SALE but so what?

The headline has to do two main things:

1. Catch the eye of that segment of the readership who are likely customers.
2. Promise them some benefit (simply offering 'x% off' or a 'Sale' is a bit of a cliché).

So in the case of the company with its burglar alarms to sell, the headline might read something like:
WORRIED ABOUT BURGLARIES?
or CROOKS AVOID THESE HOMES!
or HAVE YOU HAD A BREAK-IN?
This emphasises the point that the heading need not be short, in fact ultra short headings are very restrictive.

These examples also show two popular ways of writing a catchy headline: a) using a question and b) using a challenging, possibly puzzling, statement.

There are other clever techniques

you can employ to catch a reader's attention and attract those readers who are potential customers:

Reflect Current News Tie in the headline to a non-controversial event being reported currently in the News.

Misquote a Well-Known Phrase You might catch the reader's attention by misquoting a well-known saying, a film/book title, or a line from a song. But care must be taken from a legal point of view, so take legal advice on your proposed idea if it comes into this category.

Involve The Reader In the headline, include the reader. For example "Good Mothers..", "Have You Had a Break-In?", "Top Executives..". and so on. (Note the use of flattery and plurals too — the latter indicates that others are buying it/doing it or whatever!).

Include A Well-Known Brand A small company can increase its credibility by incorporating a well-known and prestigious company or brand name in the headline, where that product or service is being advertised. Check first with the company concerned as they will probably be sensitive about the use of their name, though on the other hand with retail advertising they may agree to contributing towards the advertising costs.

Another way of making a catchy headline (which may also be reflected in a photo) is the use of a celebrity. This, of course, must have the celebrity's specific permission which is best secured in writing.

Needs/Desires We all have needs and desires. Sometimes these are not in the forefront of our minds but a suitable headline can raise its profile and even subtly allow us to justify to ourselves that a particular desire is in fact a need!

If possible, avoid overused words such as "New, Exciting, Sale, Discount, x% off, Prices Slashed" etc. Try to be more original.

The headline, though it should be large should not be too large in relation to the surrounding words in nearby articles or in your own advert. If it is out of scale it is unlikely to be read easily. Also note that we read a mixture of upper and lower case letters better than just capitals (which is why the signs on all our main roads use upper and lower case letters).

When you have drafted several versions of a headline, test it by asking yourself (and others if possible):

1. Why would a likely customer read it?
2. What benefit is offered or hinted at?
3. Will they want to read on?

Successful advertisements are those that focus closely on those readers who are very definitely potential customers rather than a "scattershot" approach hoping that any reader might respond. Even a highly-targetted consumer or trade publication will be read by many who are not potential customers, so you should always have a picture of the potential customer in your mind and ask what would make them respond to the advertisement.

VISUALS

Display ads should, wherever possible, be illustrated with a photograph(s) or drawing(s). There are four types of illustration that can be used:

a) Photo of Product This is popular in trade publications where the application or use of the product is understood by the reader. A drawing carries less conviction but may be necessary if the product is still at the design stage or difficult to photograph in which case a professionally produced drawing may be acceptable.

b) Photo of Product/Service in Context This is a very good idea as it shows the product in use or can illustrate a service being performed. Whereas the straightforward product photo will usually have the product in front of a simple studio backdrop, the context photo is much more demanding as the context or image can have a marked bearing on the whole ad. It is particularly useful for consumer ads as it immediately gives a number of "clues" to the reader such as the age, sex, lifestyle, financial and social status of the likely user.

c) Photo of Product/Service in Unusual Context With some ingenuity you can make the product or service stand out by doing something unusual or

". . . you can't see the News for the Frees"

Advertising — How?

slightly silly. For instance you might show off your waterproof watches by photographing them in a washing machine being spun around with the clothes. Or you might illustrate the heat-retention properties of the new thermal underwear you have designed by showing a picture of people wearing only these thermal undies while waiting for a bus in winter (and standing beside others fully dressed but looking cold).

d) *Attention Getter* This could be a photo, drawing or graphics device which does not show the product or service being advertised but is there simply to catch the reader's attention.

Graphics Few small businesses will have anyone "in-house" who can produce effective graphics, unless of course the business is itself a design company! Using outside help may prove expensive, however, one possibility arises where your eye might have been caught by the use of clever graphics in a completely different context (ie outside your own business sector) where the concept or idea can be adapted to suit your own business. But note that simply copying any graphic design or drawing may be a breach of Copyright.

Be careful too that by copying in this way, particularly for a similar product or service belonging to someone else, you could be accused of attempting to mislead the public into thinking your product or service is the same as that of the original and you might be sued.

One graphics technique, often used in small newspaper display ads, is to reverse the text out of a black box (ie the ad is mainly black with white lettering). As our natural reaction is to notice light rather than dark things then this particular technique is usually not effective unless the ad is only surrounded by normal plain lineage Classified ads or editorial.

Photos A wholesaler, retailer or importer may be able to obtain suitable photographs from their suppliers. A manufacturer will need to get a professional photographer to take them. For a colour advertisement, you need a colour transparency (normally 35mm will suffice). In contrast, a black & white advert can take the image from a black & white glossy print, or a colour print or (exceptionally) from an illustration in a colour brochure if it is crystal sharp. Amateur photos usually look terrible! Remember too that a photo that looks crisp and sharp when printed on glossy magazine paper will tend to look grey and fuzzy with loss of detail when reproduced in most newspapers. This is a problem if it is the detail you are trying to show. See also the section on photos in the Chapter **Producing A Leaflet/Brochure** for more information.

Though the photo or illustration should be dominant, it need not be a plain rectangular shape. See the ideas illustrated opposite.

Typefaces The headline and all the words used in the advert will be typeset and there are literally hundreds of styles of lettering (called "typefaces") to choose from. See Chapter **Producing A Leaflet/Brochure** for more information.

BODY (SELLING) COPY

A good photo or sketch may be "worth a thousand words", but that does not mean the words are unnecessary or unimportant!

The Headline and Visuals should have selected those readers who are prospects, catching their attention however fleetingly. It is now the turn of the "Body Copy" to create sufficient interest for them to respond. How this might be done is as follows:

Put Yourself In The Reader's Place
Although the advert, one hopes, will be looked at by hundreds or thousands of people, it should be written with an individual in mind. Therefore put yourself in the shoes of the target reader and ask the sort of questions they will be asking themselves and specifically try to overcome the sales barriers they may be erecting in their minds.

But first the ad must state just *what* is being sold. This must be completely unambiguous. Will the reader be seeking detailed information at this stage? Prices? Availability? Performance? How it compares with competitors? And so on. If the reader is already using a rival's product or service, why should they change (we all tend to stick with something with which we are familiar). What objections may the reader be raising? The reader can be involved by frequent use of the word "you", by jargon or phraseology they can relate to, and perhaps by just a little flattery too!

Tell A Story The selling copy should impart some information. It should, if possible, be *new* to the reader, ie not simply stating the obvious or, as some readers may be existing customers, it should not simply state what such a customer is already likely to know as that will obviously be very boring for them. The selling copy is often written in the present, rather than future, tense to give a sense of immediacy.

HEADING   HEADING

selling message selling message selling message sel
ling message selling message selling message messag
e selling message selling message selling message s
elling message selling message selling message selli
ng message selling message selling message selling

company name & address company name &

These four scaled-down dummy fashion ads illustrate a number of options when designing a display advertisement.

(Top Left) Here the design is simply the photo with the model in the middle, a headline above, with text and address below. This is a popular format, but it is a little basic. The border thickness (called "weight") is shown here as a half point, and the photo has a fine surrounding line (a "keyline"). The keyline which acts as a barrier between the photo and the text could be removed. The design shown is also a bit dense — it needs more "white space".

(Top Right) Here the heading is "reversed out". It is balanced by the surround and the smaller black band at the base of the ad. The model is offset and the selling message is located in a white box within the photo area. Reversed out text, in moderation, is a strong visual technique.

(Bottom Left) In this ad the photo has been used to fill the entire ad space available and the heading and selling message are then superimposed over the background. Black lettering is used as the photo background is light, but on a dark background the text can be reversed out in white. For legibility, use a typeface with no fine lines and make it large enough to be clear.

(Bottom Right) Here the ad uses a close-up of the model with the background cut away (done by scalpel) so that the subject of the photo stands out and there is no distracting background. Only certain compositions lend themselves to this treatment. The white space created is used for the heading and selling message.

HEADING HEADING

selling message se
lling message selli
ng message selling
message selling m
essage selling mes
sage selling messa
ge selling message
selling message se

company name & address

Heading Heading

selling message selling mes
sage selling message selling
message selling selling mes
sage selling message selling

company name/address

Heading Heading

selling message se
lling message selling
message selling mes
sage selling mess
age selling message

company name
& address

Advertising — How?

Sell The Benefits   As detailed in the Chapter **Selling Techniques**, a customer buys benefits, not features, so it is no use relating, for instance, the clever technical design of the electrically controlled door mirrors on a car you are selling. The would-be purchaser is far more interested in the benefit that this allows, ie one can adjust the passenger door mirror from the driving seat without leaning across. He or she does not care how you achieve the mirror adjustment so long as it can be done easily!

In particular, the "unique selling proposition" of the business, which was discussed in the Introduction to this section of the book, should be stressed.

A Sales Slogan could also reflect the unique selling proposition.

Build Confidence   The reader's confidence in your company's ability to deliver the promises made in the ad can be reinforced by a variety of techniques such as the use of well-known (and reputable) brand-names; a celebrity endorsing the product or service; (in a trade context) a comment like "we already supply....(listing well-known companies)", or by citing its proven popularity (since nothing succeeds like success!).

Quite a sophisticated version is the (true) short story which may run something like "It was Friday 5.40pm, the end of another busy week, when the phone rang. It was (well-known person or company) who wanted xxxxxx (something truly huge/amazing/big order) by noon on Saturday (or some other near-impossible feat)." Then follows the amazing/humorous saga..... Dunkirk spirit...heroic tale...tears almost running down the reader's cheeks... lump in the throat etc. And of course it all has a happy and successful ending!

Avoid Hype   Having said all that, in most adverts, you should avoid hype as most readers are rather cynical about anything which is over-played and generally accompanied by lots of razzamatazz, even more so if your target readership are trade buyers.

Use the Correct Number of Words
In general, advertisers seem nervous about using too many words in an ad and tend to err on the short almost cryptic side. Equally, some writers of advertising copy seem to be attempting to win literary prizes by the lengths they write. There is obviously an optimum depending on the context. Most busy people have short attention spans, frequently flicking through magazines or skipping through newspapers. Try to use lots of short, punchy sentences, short paragraphs and paragraph headings which, like a popular newspaper, can encapsulate the message in a few words which a following paragraph can then enlarge upon.

Look at other ads of similar size in your own trade sector to get a feel for what is obviously too short or too long. Count the number of words used in these ads to get an idea as to how many words you need to aim for.

Quote Prices   Whether to show prices or not is a frequent source of debate. There are probably only two situations when prices might not be mentioned. These are when you are selling top luxury goods to those consumers who are so wealthy that they need not ask the price, and the other situation is when you are selling large capital cost equipment where the end price depends on too many details or variations to be able to quote a price in an advert. Otherwise, the balance is probably in favour of quoting your prices — after all, most of us want to know what it is going to cost us. The omission of a price does tend to create an impression that things are very expensive. Note that where prices are shown, there must be no hidden extra costs, eg if postage is always charged, it must be shown prominently.

If you are unsure about quoting a price because, quite frankly, your prices are uncompetitive, then that is a separate issue which needs resolving first!

CALL FOR ACTION

As we are concerned here with response advertisements, we must include a call for action. This point cannot be over-stressed. Most people live busy lives and need a gentle push to get them to overcome the standard reaction "That looks interesting, but I'll see to it tommorow/next week/next month" (ie never!). Hence a closing line must involve a *date* and/or *time* after which the reader will be disappointed, or you might hint at scarcity. Examples are: "Limited offer ends Saturday 3rd June" or "New Stock from France will be arriving Monday 15th May" or "Have only managed to persuade the overseas makers to let us have 135 for Britain and these will be sold strictly on a first-come, first-served basis with no queue-jumping!" or "Last 4 left in Britain" or "Beat the Budget — buy before 31st March" or "Prices rising on 1st September, buy now and save £x". Note the closing line must be true!

An alternative strategy is to link the call for action to another benefit, eg a discount or gift for all purchases made before a certain date. Or visit on such-

and-such a date and meet some well-known celebrity.

Another very effective technique is the coupon which the reader is encouraged to complete and return. This should be simple to complete with a big enough space to write in. It should request BLOCK CAPITALS and could use a Freepost reply (see the item on Direct Mail in the Chapter **Sorting Out The Sales Distribution**).

By this time you may be thinking — how on earth am I supposed to meet all these demanding requirements? It certainly may appear daunting at first sight, for producing effective ads does require some effort and some practice. But take heart in the fact that for the ad to be effective does not require every detail to be spot on, it just helps if it is. With some practice the techniques will begin to come more naturally — after all, they are really quite logical.

NAME & ADDRESS

After getting the reader interested in what you are offering, you need to tell them how to get it! The key question to ask yourself is how are people likely to contact you — by phone, by letter, by fax, by telex, in person or at an Exhibition? The name and address block in the advert need not simply be a copy of your formal letterhead address. If most customers are likely to contact you by phone then the telephone number should be dominant. In contrast, if you are a retailer and people have no reason to phone, then why waste space with a phone number?

If people are likely to visit your premises which are tucked away, then a small map indicating the nearest car park and, where relevant, tube station,

"Turn right here...whoops!
I'm sure that ad said......"

would be more useful. Alternatively if there is a well-known landmark nearby, you might simply state something like "Find us opposite the Theatre Royal".

In any event the address part of the ad should not normally take up more than a third of the space (in the case of a very small ad) but considerably less with a larger ad. The ultimate error is to give a company name and forget the address altogether.....which does sometimes happen!

Details As in every aspect of business it is the little details that count, and ads are no exception:

Hours If your business works unusual hours or is to be open during a Holiday period, this should be mentioned so that potential business is not lost.

Phone Orders If you are able to take orders over the phone, perhaps with the customer using a credit card, then again this could be mentioned. It all makes life easier for the customer and they are therefore more likely to respond.

Credit Facilities If the cost of your product or service is such that a greater number of people may be able to afford it if credit facilities are available then you might mention this (but for non-trade customers, note the legal requirements of the Consumer Credit Act — which also controls how credit offers are shown in an ad). For details, contact your local Trading Standards Officer (or Consumer Protection or Weights & Measures Officer). It is a criminal offence to give credit without a licence unless you are exempt.

Crowding Do not be tempted to fill every corner of your advert space. Allow some "white space", as it is called, to let the important details stand out.

Accuracy Do be sure the spelling is right and that your address and phone/fax number is correct. Also ensure all details (such as prices) are accurate as an error there may constitute an offence.

OTHER POINTS

Paid Advertisement A special and very effective form of the display ad is a page or half page that *looks* like a normal article and is written like an article except it is an advertisement. It will have the words "Advertisement" or "Paid Advertisement" or something similar, usually at the top. Done well this is a very good way to get your message across, though you need to ensure readers understand it is an ad.

Advertising — How?

Advertising Agencies As your business grows larger and your advertising budget becomes quite large, say over £30,000-£50,000, then you may consider appointing an Advertising Agency. Their functions can be all or just part of the following:

1. To carry out background market research
2. To conceive advertising campaign themes
3. To research which media to use
4. To create the ads
5. To place the ads, as cheaply as possible, for their client

Advertising Agencies often charge *both* their clients and the medium which is carrying the advertisement. They usually charge a consumer publication 15% and a trade publication 10% of the advertisement cost, and in addition they can make production and other charges on the client.

If you plan to use an Advertising Agency, key points to remember are: a) fix a definite "not to exceed" budget and b) produce a clear and well-defined brief as to your objectives.

DESIGNING CLASSIFIED ADS

An important difference between display and classified ads is that with a display ad you are trying to catch the attention of a reader who is not necessarily in a buying mood. In contrast those people who read the Classified columns are actively seeking something.

There are 4 parts to a good Classified ad, which are:

1. The Headline
2. Selling Copy (ie the words)
3. Call for Action
4. Name & Address/Phone Number

Most publications allow only a brief Headline which is in bold letters at the start of the ad. This is usually restricted to two or three words, so unlike a display ad you need to be specific, mentioning precisely what is on offer.

Then with the Selling Copy as you are limited for space, you need to emphasise the benefits. There is often little space for details. A Call for Action is as essential as with a display ad and can use similar wording.

Finally, to save space you should only provide the minimum (appropriate) business name and address details.

Remember that all trade Classified ads must indicate clearly that they are in fact trade advertisements. Using the business name in addition to a phone number or address usually covers this point.

When To Use A Classified Ad

Classified ads are often used in the following circumstances. First by businesses that need to continually advertise their services (eg plumbers, joiners, tyre repairers etc). Sheer cost would probably prevent them using larger display ads and those people who need their services will often scan the Classified columns.

The next category that use Classified ads are small businesses who need to promote some special event, eg an end-of-Season Sale, but who cannot afford display advertising. In general, low-price bargains are favourites for the Classified columns.

A good technique is to use several small ads in the same issue of a publication rather than one long ad. Another point is if the publication lists Classified ads alphabetically, choose a headline with a letter starting A or B!

PLACING THE AD

This is sometimes referred to as "booking space". As soon as you know the desired timing of the ads you wish to place, contact the Advertising Department(s) of the publication(s) or broadcast media and make your booking. The details you will need to cover include:

Price It is always worth trying to negotiate a discount. This is very common especially with smaller publications. One simple strategy is to request the same percentage discount they would have to offer an Advertising Agency. Another strategy if advertising for the first time, is to ask if they will give a discount to encourage you to try advertising with them.

If you are not supplying camera ready artwork (as described in the next Chapter), ask if there is any charge for typesetting and laying out your advert. This should be a nominal figure unless you want something fancy. Remember that most people will quote prices which exclude VAT (which must be added).

Payment Terms Establish what the terms are. Usually a short period of credit (up to 30 days) is allowed.

Position With publications it is essential to discuss where the ad will be placed. The ideal place is usually a right hand page (in the bottom right corner if your ad is only part of the page) and facing an article (ie "facing matter" as this is called) rather than somebody else's full page ad. It is usually better to be in the early part of a publication, unless you want your ad to be near some special feature which occurs later in the issue. Sometimes there is a small extra charge for specifying the position. If offered "ROP" this means the ad will

PRODUCING A RADIO COMMERCIAL

You do not have to be a big business to use commercial radio. In fact commercial radio can be an effective advertising medium for a wide range of consumer and business orientated products.

Radio Audiences Over three quarters of all adults own a portable radio or radio/cassette player and well over half of all households have a radio or radio/cassette player in their car. The radio is also used in many work places. In any given area of the country typically between one third and one half the adult population will listen regularly to a local commercial radio station. The audience figures are therefore very large. People listen to radio for a variety of reasons — company, entertainment, background music and information. Sometimes the context is one where any advertisement has to catch the listener's attention. But some audiences, eg car drivers, are "captive", ie unable to look at or listen to other media because of what they are doing.

The measurement of radio audiences is done by JICRAR (The Joint Industry Committee for Radio Audience Research). Samples of listeners keep diaries in which they record full details of their listening habits. This information is available from the local radio sales staff and is vitally important to would-be advertisers.

One of the key findings of JICRAR research is that the vast majority of radio listening is habitual, ie listeners tune in at the same time irrespective of the particular programme on the air. This points to the need to spread your radio spots time-wise to reach the maximum number of listeners. But for targetting specific listeners such as business people the drive-to-work times of 7-9am and 4-6pm are ideal (these times can be extended in the South-East) while morning programmes are listened to by many housewives. There may be a small surcharge for your ad to be broadcast during specific times.

Costs Costs are based on air-time (ie quoted as £ for a 10, 20 or 30 second slot). As a rule of thumb you need to add 10% for production costs. The details will be provided in a Rate Card just like any other media. Stations broadcasting to major conurbations such as London, Manchester, Birmingham or Glasgow charge more for a given slot than a station broadcasting to a small rural community.

Market research indicates that the typical length of a radio commercial (ie 10, 20 or 30 seconds) makes little difference to its impact. So choose as short a slot as your message requires.

Although as little as 14 spots a week may constitute an effective campaign in terms of coverage, more spots would normally be advised to build up awareness, either by extending the duration of the campaign to more than one week or having more spots in the week.

Production Before considering how your own ad should sound, listen to other ads and note what sounds good, what catches your attention and who else is advertising. Most local radio stations can offer a creative service to help you to produce the commercial. This is important to ensure a professional ad which also complies with all relevant legalities. A common mistake is to try to squeeze in too many words. In a 30 second slot which finishes with a very brief jingle, there is only time for about 100 words, spoken quickly! The other popular style which has a jingle at the beginning and end (called a "top and tail") can reduce the time for words in the middle down to 30-50 words. Interestingly, research shows that commercials with dialogue achieve higher impact than a single voice.

The radio station will have "library music" which you can make use of for a charge. A "jingle" is where a composer produces a specific piece of music just for your ad and grants you a licence to use it for one or two years. Though this may cost £500+ it is exclusive and you save on the charges for using library music.

If possible, ask for a "demo commercial". This will cost extra but you can hear how the ad should sound.

Information produced with the kind assistance of Radio Clyde

Advertising — How?

be placed anywhere in the "run of the paper".

With broadcast media, the day and time when the commercial is to be broadcast is as crucial. With local radio, the drive-to-work times of 7-9am and 4-6pm have a good audience of business people, while morning programmes are listened to by housewives.

Artwork If the publication is doing the artwork, find out what they need and by what date. Also ask what charge they are going to make, as some publications do this free while others make charges. Ask to see a proof of your ad. If supplying the artwork yourself, you will need to know the "mechanical data", ie what size the ad should be, what screen size for any photos and if the artwork is to be supplied as positive or negative film. It is really most important that you provide the artwork to the exact dimensions as specified by the publication.

Deadlines It is essential to know what the deadlines are. These will be different depending upon whether you are producing the artwork for the ad or not. There are also usually different deadlines for colour ads, mono ads and Classified.

Voucher Copy Ensure your ad is booked in the correct issue and request you are sent a free "voucher" copy.

Confirmation It is probably prudent to confirm everything in a letter or fax.

MONITORING YOUR ADS

Far too few businesses (large or small) make enough of an attempt to monitor the results of their advertising. In fact, if there was more monitoring, the present structure and style of most advertising would probably change markedly. A small business really cannot afford to waste money on non-effective advertising.

By careful design of their ads and by close monitoring of the results, the effectiveness can be measured and future advertising fine-tuned. Not all strategies work well for everyone everywhere. It is useful to find out which ones work and which do not. You might even discover that advertising does not prove to be effective for your particular business and your budget is better spent on other promotional activity, such as PR.

Monitoring

How can this monitoring be done? There are, of course, many ways depending on the circumstances, but they all boil down to 3 basic approaches:

a) Reply By Post Whenever the reader replies by post it is relatively easy to monitor the advert response. If advertising in more than one publication, you can make small changes to the address so that you can tell from which ad the response emanates. The use of "Dept X" at the start of an address is rather hackneyed. But what about using fictitious room numbers "Room 3" or fictitious persons "Mr Smith" at the start of the address to indicate which publication. If you are asking the reader to complete and return a coupon it is even easier to monitor the response with a reference code printed on the coupon.

b) Bring A Coupon Where the reader is required to visit you (as in a retail context), then a coupon which promises some benefit, ie a gift or a discount, will give an idea of response.

c) Direct Question The reader may be responding by phone, in which case the fictitious person approach may still be used if the ad says "Please phone and ask for Miss Smith". Or you might ask how the caller heard about you. In a person-to-person situation (such as in a shop or when selling to a business), simply asking the respondent where they heard about your product or service will usually provide the information you require.

In practice this has to be done using some sort of little routine, otherwise it is easily forgotten. One suggestion is to print or photocopy small cards which simply list the different ways a person might hear about you, eg through your various ads; mentions in the Press; by word of mouth or other means. After each person is asked, the correct box is ticked on the card — with one card being used per person. Depending upon your type of business, these cards could be held by a cash-till (in a shop) or beside a phone or whatever.

"I hired this uniform as I thought it was a TV commercial!"

Advertising – How?

What Should An Advert Earn?

It is quite sobering to calculate how many sales your ads need to generate simply to cover their cost. This can be estimated approximately as follows:

First you need to know what the Gross Margin of your business is.

$$\text{Gross Margin} = \frac{\text{Gross Profit (excl VAT)}}{\text{Total Sales (excl VAT)}}$$

As an example, assume these figures are:

$$\text{Gross Margin} = \frac{£22,174}{£51,738} = 43\%$$

Then the gross profit from £100 of sales (or £85.11 net of 17.5% VAT) is:

$$£85.11 \times 0.43 = £36.60$$

So if an advertisement cost £150 + VAT, then the amount of additional sales (including VAT) this would need to generate for this example is:

$$\frac{150}{36.60} \times £100 = £410$$

This is of course just an approximate figure but it does serve as a reminder as to just how much extra sales you have to generate to cover your ad costs.

SOME LEGAL POINTS

There are a very large number of laws, regulations and Codes of Practice governing advertising. For instance:

Misleading Advertisements The Control of Misleading Advertisement Regulations 1988 gives the Director General of Fair Trading the power to stop an advertisement. The word "advertisement" in these Regulations includes newspaper and magazine ads, outdoor advertising (eg bus sides and posters), cinema commercials, leaflets, brochures, inserts, display material, point of sale ads, circulars and direct mail. It excludes TV and cable TV (under the Independent TV Commission, tel: 071-255 3000) and radio (under the Radio Authority, tel: 071-430 2724).

For the purposes of these Regulations an advertisement is defined as misleading as follows: if in any way, including its presentation, it deceives or is likely to deceive the persons to whom it is addressed or whom it reaches and if, by reason of its deceptive nature, it is likely to affect their economic behaviour or, for those reasons, injures or is likely to injure a competitor of the person whose interests the advertisement seeks to promote.

An advertisement can be misleading where, for example, it contains a false statement of fact, conceals or leaves out important facts, or promises to do something but there is no intention of carrying it out.

Other Regulations & Laws There are also other important regulations and laws which affect advertising such as the Trade Descriptions Act and Consumer Credit Act. These are normally enforced by Trading Standards (or Consumer Protection) Departments. There is also legislation specific to many trade sectors.

British Code of Advertising Practice To assist advertisers, the Committee of Advertising has produced a Code which provides excellent and detailed advice. A copy of the Code (which is in the form of a slim booklet) is available from the Advertising Standards Authority Ltd, Brook House, 2-16 Torrington Place, London WC1E 7HN. Tel: 071-580 5555.

Mail Order Not surprisingly, the Code covers Mail Order and Direct Response Advertising in some depth.

In addition there are now specific rules for mailing lists and database management.

Sales Promotion The Committee of Advertising Practice also produce a detailed booklet entitled "The British Code of Sales Promotion Practice" which covers, for instance: premium offers of all kinds; reduced price and free offers; the distribution of vouchers, coupons and samples; personality promotions; sales & trade incentive promotions etc.

Finally, all advertisements and sales promotions should be *"legal, decent, honest and truthful"* ■

---

10 Common Errors When Advertising

1. Assuming that one big ad is all that is necessary to let potential customers know what is on offer.
2. Placing an ad simply in response to pressure from an advertising sales person.
3. Advertising in the wrong place.
4. Spending too little on advertising when monitoring indicates it is achieving a satisfactory response.
5. Advertising without a clear idea as to its purpose.
6. Using your business name for the ad headline (only sometimes is this valid).
7. Designing an 'image' ad, then expecting a response.
8. Omitting a clear 'Call for Action' at the end of an ad.
9. Placing an ad too hastily.
10. Continuing to place ads without monitoring the results.

Producing A Leaflet/Brochure

Many businesses produce a leaflet, pamphlet, brochure or catalogue and such a publication can be an integral part of their marketing campaign.

Unfortunately, many leaflets, pamphlets etc are produced without any precise objective in mind and are all too often little more than ego trips. Too much attention is given to what they look like rather than what they are supposed to achieve. A leaflet, pamphlet etc is nothing more than a specialised form of advertisement and should be thought of as such.

Just to clarify the terminology, a leaflet is, strictly speaking, a single sheet of printed matter whereas a pamphlet, brochure or catalogue consists of several sheets. In practice these words are often used interchangeably. In this Chapter these are all referred to simply as "leaflets".

The decision to produce a leaflet will stem from considerations of the many different ways of advertising as covered in the Chapter **Advertising – Why? Where? When?** The fundamental questions to answer are: a) what is the purpose of the leaflet (ie what will be gained from producing it); b) who is the target reader; c) how will the leaflet be distributed and d) what is the budget for the project? Let us look at these questions in more detail:

Purpose Leaflets fall into two broad categories – those that introduce a new product or service to a likely customer and those that turn an already interested customer into a buyer. An example of the first category would be a leaflet delivered through your door; an example of the second category would be a leaflet given to you on your request at an Exhibition.

Since the first category is a cold sale it must be much more *persuasive* and *brief*. The second category is being read by someone who is already interested and will therefore be at the stage of requiring sufficient *details* to make a purchasing decision.

The first category also needs to be produced and distributed in much larger quantities than the second category as the response rate to any cold selling approach will be much lower. This has implications in terms of the unit printing cost of the leaflet you are considering (more of which below).

Just what can a leaflet achieve which other forms of advertising and promotion cannot? The obvious point is that your leaflet will at least be looked at without the competition for attention from other advertisements or articles in a publication. Leaflets allow much more space for words and pictures than you can normally afford with an ad and you can, to some extent, control who receives them. In particular they are useful in face-to-face selling situations as they back-up the sales pitch and allow the salesperson to leave the product or service details with the potential buyer.

Target Reader As with any form of advertising it is crucial to continually place yourself in the shoes of the people who are likely to read the leaflet. Will it catch the person's eye? Will it relate to them and their needs? Will they even want to read it? Will it encourage them to take the next step towards making a purchase?

Try to avoid a layout which is either difficult to follow or one that is more concerned about stating how wonderful and marvellous the company or its products/services are. Keep thinking about the target customers, who are really more interested in themselves and will be thinking "what's in this for me?".

Distribution Obviously it is no good having an excellent leaflet if you cannot distribute them effectively. The distribution method will have implications for the leaflet design, ie if being sent by post it must fit an envelope or if it is a loose insert in a magazine it must suit the publication's own requirements. Different distribution methods are discussed later in this Chapter.

Budget A leaflet can range from a cheap ⅓rd A4 size piece of paper printed on thin paper right up to a full-colour multipage heavyweight booklet! Probably both extremes should be avoided, ie it should not be a skimped unprofessional document that gives an unfavourable impression of the business nor a glossy heavyweight doorstop!

A useful guide is to look at what your competitors are producing. The best rule is to produce the least elaborate leaflet which is likely to achieve its objective. You must not think that the likely result in terms of sales is proportional to the cost of the publication. The requirements for your own leaflet will hopefully become clearer as this Chapter unfolds.

PRINTING A LEAFLET
If you are going to have a leaflet printed (and probably a number of such publications printed over the years) it makes sense to have at least a basic understanding of how printing is done so that the leaflet you produce not only accurately reflects your ideas but has been printed as economically as possible.

GLOSSARY OF PRINTING

A3,A4,A5 — Paper sizes. A4 = 210 x 297mm. A3 is twice the size of A4 and A5 is half A4 in size.

Artwork — See "Camera ready artwork".

Assembly — Multipage or colour printing requires a number of sheets of film to be "assembled" accurately in the correct positions before printing can begin.

Bleed — This is where a photograph or a tinted area goes off the edge of the paper.

Bromide — A photographic paper on which the typeset text (and sometimes the half-tone illustrations) appear as an intermediate stage in the printing process.

Camera ready artwork — Text, drawings etc prepared to a final state so they look exactly as they will appear on the final leaflet.

Copy — The words of an advert or leaflet in either manuscript or typed form before they are typeset.

Cromalin — A colour proof of a full colour ad/leaflet. It is Du Pont's brand name but is often used to describe any colour proof.

Crop — To crop a photo is to indicate which part of the photo is to appear (ie you do not need to print the whole area of a photo). It does not involve cutting the photo!

Dupe Tranny — Slang for a "duplicate colour transparency".

Film — A photographic sheet, the size of the page or advert. Produced by photographing the camera ready artwork and needed to make the printing plates.

Full Colour — All full colour printing is done using the three "process colours" and black, ie only four inks.

Galley — Term sometimes used for the long length of typeset text usually one column of text wide, ready for "paste-up".

Gsm — Grams per square metre. Used to describe the weight of paper. (Indicates its thickness).

Half Tone — Black & white photos or other illustrations which include shades of grey, after they have been "screened".

Imposition — Only relevant with a multipage brochure. It refers to the positioning of the different pages on the assembly film so that when printed on a large single sheet of paper, the pages all appear in the correct sequence when folded.

Justified Text — Text which has both its left and right margin edges straight (like the columns in this book).

Laminating — A finishing process which puts a glossy transparent surface on a leaflet or menu. See also "Varnishing".

Landscape — Where a photo or illustration is a *horizontal* rectangle (like a landscape painting). The opposite, "portrait", is vertical.

Leading — The space between lines of text — measured in "points".

Letterpress — A type of printing, now mainly superseded by Offset Litho for most leaflets and brochures.

Line Drawings — Graphs, tables or sketches with only black lines.

Mono — Monotone, ie one colour, usually black.

NCR — No Carbon Required. A type of paper used for invoices etc which is impregnated with carbon particles which break when written or typed upon, so no carbon paper required.

Offset Litho — A popular type of printing often used for leaflets etc.

Origination — A general term to describe the preparation of camera ready artwork.

Ozalid — Brand name for a type of page proof.

Pantone — Brand name for a popular printer's colour chart.

Paste-up — The camera ready artwork produced by pasting the galleys, illustrations etc in their correct positions on a sheet.

Plate — This is a thin metal, plastic or stiff paper sheet, produced either photographically from "film" or direct from the camera ready artwork. Fitted onto the printing machine.

Point Size — A printer's unit of measurement. Used for the size of text and the "Leading". 1 point = 0.3515mm.

Process colours — Magenta, cyan and yellow are called process colours. Combined with black they can reproduce almost any colour.

Proof — The camera ready artwork (or a photocopy of it), or a "pull" to check before the leaflet is printed.

Reduction — A normal photographic process to reduce artwork/photos.

Repro — A word sometimes used to describe the scanning and assembly work, mainly relevant to full colour printing.

Retouching — This is a skilled (and usually expensive) process where an artist changes minor details of a photo.

Reverse Out — Having text or an image reversed out of the ink, ie on white paper with black ink, the text appears in white.

Scanning — To produce the "separations" from a colour photo or artwork requires a special laser to scan the colour image.

Screening — This photographic process converts grey shades in a black & white photo into black dots. Far apart dots give a light grey, closer together they give a darker grey. Screening can also be used with spot colour to lighten the shade.

Separations — These are 4 sheets of film, produced photographically. One for each of the 3 process colours and black that together make a colour image, as required for full colour printing.

Spot Colour — The use of a colour to brighten up or highlight an otherwise black & white print. Quite cheap to do. You can have more than one spot colour.

Stitching — Putting one or two wire staples into the spine of a brochure. Also called "saddle-stitching".

Tints — The grey shading on this page is a simple example.

Typeface — The different styles of print. There are hundreds in use but any printer will only have a selection.

Typesetting — This is the process of setting the type to produce the galleys ready for paste-up.

Varnishing — A coating that gives a glossy transparent appearance similar to laminating.

Producing A Leaflet/Brochure

Modern technology permits today's printers to produce products of astonishing variety and complexity. The innocent question "Is it possible to do..." will often be answered "Yes" but the cost might not be appreciated when you see the final bill!

The printing industry is very old and so has evolved a language of its own, the commonly used words of which are translated on the previous page.

DESIGNING A LEAFLET

Quite a number of decisions need to be made to design a leaflet. An early decision is whether or not it should be in colour.

Colour Full colour is expensive but it is justified if the product or service you are offering is itself expensive or needs colour to show its features (eg a wallpaper leaflet or a brochure of knitwear would be difficult to produce effectively in anything other than full colour). Another justification for using full colour may be if you need to compete head-on with a rival's brochure which is also in full colour.

There is a steady increase in the use of full colour for all types of printed material so your readers are becoming more and more used to reading full colour publications. This means that more leaflets are likely to need to be printed in full colour in the future.

A cheaper alternative to full colour might be the use of two or even three colours. This can be quite effective especially if large heading letters or a decorative band is printed in a screened colour which lightens the tone and gives the effect of another colour. This can look more sophisticated than bold brassy colours. You might also consider using full colour in only part of a leaflet or you might try using coloured paper (see below).

Size The size of the leaflet, in terms of its physical dimensions and number of pages, is a function of the amount of information you need to convey, the intended method of distribution and, of course, the size of your budget. Several typical sizes are: A4, A4 folded in two or three, A5 and one third A4.

Any of these can be printed on one or both sides. Of course they need not be exactly A5, A4 or whatever but such standardisation is usually economical.

A point for consideration is that leaflets which are free and which we receive unsolicited (and hence might discard) are often exactly one of these 'standard' sizes, so you might choose a non-standard size to be different.

Paper The thickness and quality of paper is an important factor as the leaflet will be handled by the recipient. A thin or coarse paper feels cheap while a stiff smooth paper gives a feeling of quality. Paper weights are expressed in grams per square metre, gsm for short, and typically 80-100gsm is about as light as one would risk for a leaflet, 130gsm is common while 150 gsm is quite stiff. The finish to the paper can be matt, semi-matt or glossy. A small but not insignificant aspect to watch is that some "white" papers are in fact quite off-white in colour.

A printer will usually show you a paper sample which is a blank sheet. To the uninitiated it is very difficult to assess how such a paper will look and feel when it is printed on. Ask if they have an example of that paper printed for someone else. Alternatively, find someone else's leaflet, the paper of which you like, and then ask the printer to match it.

Instead of (or in addition to) using coloured ink you might choose to print the leaflet on a coloured, patterned or textured paper. This requires some caution to do effectively. A bright red, blue or yellow paper looks, frankly, rather garish, even cheap and a more subtle tone such as light grey or creamy paper could look super in the right context. Obviously a fashion or very consumer-orientated leaflet can afford to be more flamboyant than a serious trade-orientated leaflet.

Information Precisely the same rules apply as per designing Display Advertisements (see Chapter **Advertising – How?**) except that here you have the space to say and show more. But that is no excuse to ramble!

Remember to "sell the benefits" and emphasise the "unique selling proposition" of your business. One should not forget a "call for action" either.

One very important point to watch is while any ad has a relatively short life, you frequently want a leaflet to last much longer, ie you may still want to be able to issue the leaflet a year or more after it was printed. You therefore have to avoid incorporating details which are going to date it quickly. Prices in particular change, so many firms print a separate price list on cheap paper.

Where a portion of your customers are non-English speaking, consider translating at least part of the leaflet. This is obviously cheaper than printing a completely different leaflet in a foreign language.

Design For a leaflet to achieve maximum effect the overall design of the leaflet ought to be good. If you are inexperienced in this, a good way to start is to look at other people's leaflets (not simply in your own trade, but *any* leaflets) and see which designs you like best. Then take inspiration from those features you like.

If the leaflet consists of more than one page it will need to be folded, which is best done by the printers, who do this mechanically. If it consists of more than one sheet they may need to be stapled together. As a final touch the leaflet could be varnished or laminated to give a high gloss finish. This is quite expensive but looks good and resists finger marks which are a particular problem if your leaflet has large solid areas of black or other dark colours. Another problem with borders or edges of solid black or dark colours is that if folded the white base paper usually shows through at the fold line, which can be a little unsightly.

Typefaces & Typesetting Different styles of lettering are known as "typefaces". Some common ones are:

'Univers', a popular typeface, in which this sentence is set. It has clean, modern lines.

'Helvetica', in which this is set, looks very similar to 'Univers'.

This sentence is typeset in another popular typeface called 'Times New Roman' which is very conventional.

These standard typefaces are also usually available in **bold**, *italic* and sometimes in outline forms. There are also more exotic typefaces too. All lettering can be printed in different sizes, called the "point size". This text is in 8 point and is a bit small to read, while this text is in 10 point (as is most of this book), and finally this is in 12 point.

Photographs First some general rules. A good photograph must be in sharp focus and the subject of the photo must be well positioned and large enough so the reader can see whatever details are relevant. Photos should also indicate a sense of scale and having people in the scene is one way to achieve this. A small product might be shown close-up held in someone's hand to give it scale.

As humans we respond most to photos showing people rather than inanimate objects. As the people in the photo (who may be yourself, your staff and/or your customers) are unlikely to be models, care is needed to get the right feel to the finished shot with a happy, positive, professional look or whatever facial expressions are relevant in the context.

They say a camera never lies, but any photographer will tell you this is nonsense as you can photograph a scene which is contrived, or at least carefully selected, to achieve almost any effect you wish! For instance, houses which are for sale seem to be always pictured on bright sunny days, shops are always photographed as busy, travel brochures either show empty beaches (when they are usually crowded) or busy hotels (when they are often deserted)! However, the photo must not be misleading.

Always use a good professional photographer as a second-rate photo can totally spoil a leaflet.

When you commission a photographer to take your photos, note that to set up a scene, get the lighting right, place any props and backdrop, take a

Illustration shows Jaguar E-Type photo mounted with crop lines indicating which part of the photo is to be printed in the leaflet. The horse droppings in the foreground are omitted!

Producing A Leaflet/Brochure

Polaroid shot to check all is well and then actually take a series of photos, can take several hours! If using human models, it is a useful precaution to get them to sign a Release Form (the photographer may have some standard forms). This permits you to use the photographs for whatever you have specified on the form.

Black & White   To print a mono photo, the original can be either a black & white photo, a colour photo (or "print") or a photo in another leaflet, which you have permission to use. If you only have a black & white negative you will first need to get a print made, usually 6x8 or 5x7 inches in size. The photograph should be taped at its edges to a piece of blank paper and the crop lines shown to indicate which area of the photo you actually want in your leaflet. The printer will enlarge or reduce the image to suit the space available (and your wishes). This "cropping", as it is called, is illustrated on the previous page.

A problem with some leaflets is the photos appear grey, flat and gloomy. This can be for a number of reasons, such as the screen size, quality of paper used or the way in which the artwork is prepared prior to printing. Or it might simply reflect the quality of the initial photo.

Colour   To print an illustration in colour requires an original which is a colour transparency or a colour print. The transparency is usually the preferred option. Before printing can commence the colour picture must be "scanned" and then "assembled" into "separations" (see the Glossary on page 73). Be sure you get several different quotes for this and it includes producing a colour proof for you to check. The end result is four sheets of film (normally positives) showing the image and text in their correct positions and size with each film representing one of the four printing colours (black, cyan, magenta and yellow). It surprises many people that each of the four colour separations is in fact just a black image!   The separations all have alignment marks printed on them and an important task for the printer is to ensure that each colour is printed in register with the next – even a tiny error produces a fuzzy image. Any full colour leaflet is printed using only a combination of the four printing colour inks.

If you only need to produce a 100 or so leaflets, an alternative to consider is to use photo labels – these are colour photos with self-adhesive backing that you stick into spaces left on your (black & white) leaflet. The photo labels are made from your original photos and come in different sizes. One supplier of photo labels is Quadrant Processing on tel: 0527 871648.

Another idea is to use full colour photocopies which are ideal for small quantities of leaflets.

CHOOSING A PRINTER

For a relatively simple one or 2-colour leaflet, the High Street instant print shops are worth approaching for a quote. Full colour printing is more specialised and may require the services of a larger printer – see your Yellow Pages.

For some black & white leaflets, eg Price Lists, a quick and cheap way to "print" your leaflet is to get it typeset in the usual way but then to photocopy it rather than print the number you need.

For normal printing, to assess a printer's capabilities, ask to see other leaflets they have printed recently. Before a printer can give you a sensible quotation, they will need to know the following details:

1. The size (ie dimensions) of the leaflet you propose (A5, A4 or whatever).
2. The number of pages in each leaflet (if more than one).
3. The number of colours.
4. The type of paper.
5. The amount of typesetting required.
6. The number of photos (if any).
7. What finishing is required (ie folding, collating, stitching, varnishing or laminating).
8. The quantity of leaflets you need.

One thing you will need to know is how long it will take the printers to do the job. A constant source of friction between printers and their clients is the delivery time. Leaflets are often delivered late but, in fairness, clients all too frequently submit their material in a shambolic state . . . . and late too!

You must get proofs from the printer and it is sensible to look at them very carefully as mistakes can slip through. Most people, especially when they are busy, read very quickly and the brain does not simply read what it sees but rather cleverly reads what it thinks it ought to see. One example is an extra word at the end of any line may not be be spotted unless you read the proofs slowly.

Mistakes spotted on a proof should be corrected using unambiguous symbols which a printer will recognise. Some of the more common ones are given in the box (overpage).

DISTRIBUTING A LEAFLET

This should not be an after-thought but part of the decision that initially concluded a leaflet should be produced. Some of the different ways leaflets can be distributed are as listed over the page (in alphabetical order).

DESIGNING A LEAFLET   (Note: The actual leaflet's size in this example would be ⅓rd A4)

The headline promises a nice benefit and may therefore catch the attention of more prospective customers than a specific heading eg "Garden Furniture".

Photos and illustrations are more convincing than words. Ensure scenes are lively and include people.

An introductory comment is required which clearly explains what is on offer.

The main part elaborates on the offer. Remember to add prices and give enough product information to arouse interest.

A call for action by an incentive is always useful, but may date the leaflet.

If space permits you might advertise more of your range but never jeopardise the main offer by over-crowding.

Your business name would not normally be given emphasis unless it is particularly descriptive as to what you do.

This leaflet would probably require printing in full colour to maximise its impact.

A little white space helps avoid the cramped, crowded look.

If your leaflet has a lot of text, it is important to arrange it in well spaced blocks so that it is easy to read. Prospective customers will not stop to read text which needs deciphering.

A map may be important when you are not located in a town centre site or are hard to find.

If you have a business slogan or motto you could add it.

Make the most of Summer with your Family and Friends

(space for colour photo, which extends under the heading above to create a large splash of colour. In this example the photo might show the furniture outside in the sun with a few happy people around and the heading above could be printed over the sky).

Garden Furniture — Huge Selection!

We can now offer a complete choice of attractive, comfortable and yet affordable garden furniture in pine, aluminium or plastic. Elegantly designed and carefully made to be enjoyed and admired. Chairs from £19.95, tables from £49.95.

Special Offer: 20% discount if you bring this leaflet and buy at least one table and 4 chairs before 31st May 1993.

We also stock a full range of pots, potting mixes, tools, seed, hoses, fertilisers, gravel, seedling trays, sprays, plants, greenhouses........

John Smith Garden Centre
Rose Street, Anytown
Tel: 071-234 567

For the Greenest of Gardens

(Fictitious Example)

Producing A Leaflet/Brochure

Mark Made In Margin	Corresponding Mark Made In Text
✗	Encircle letters or marks to be removed. Or other error
℘	Line through letters to be deleted
⊔⊔ or italic	Straight underline letters to be _italic_
⌇⌇ or bold	Wavy underline letters to be **bold**
≡ or caps	Three underline letters to be CAPITALS
≠ or lower case	ENCIRCLE LETTERS TO BE lower case.
⌒	Close up text
⋏	word mark means insert here
⌐	move this text to the right so it is in line

Advert Response This is a neat way to allow a small advert to provide more information by inviting the reader to write or phone for a (usually free) leaflet. It also allows the reader to get more information without feeling committed. This is quite an important aspect in itself. Monitoring of the advert response is also quite easy.

Consumer Shows Since not everyone at such a show is a potential buyer, you might wish to restrict the availability of leaflets on your stand. Shows allow you the opportunity of distributing a large number of leaflets, if you wish.

Direct Mail This is an obvious place for using a leaflet. See also the item on Direct Mail in the Chapter **Sorting Out The Sales Distribution**.

Include With Invoice etc If the weight of your standard envelope and invoice is under 60 grams which is the Post Office's present minimum price/weight point, then there is scope to include a small leaflet at no extra postage cost and targeted at existing customers. It can be very effective, but only if the person who is likely to open the letter is a decision maker and appropriate to your business.

Inserts Leaflets can be enclosed inside a newspaper or magazine. Sometimes they are loose and sometimes they are bound-in. The practice is particularly common with trade magazines. The cost depends normally on the weight of the leaflet and the quantity you want distributed. Sometimes there are size or weight restrictions. It is a very cheap way of distributing a leaflet (much cheaper than posting them out individually) provided the publication's readership matches your own market.

Letterboxes This is a good way for many consumer-orientated products or services. See the item on Direct Mail in the Chapter **Sorting Out The Sales Distribution**.

Other Places There may be places where your target readers congregate and are possibly seeking information. For example, a Hotel lobby is a good place for leaflets aimed at tourists; Tourist Information Centres too; Travel Agencies for travellers; Sports Centres for sports enthusiasts. Some of these outlets will allow you to leave your leaflets at no charge, others may request commission or some other legitimate financial incentive.

Retail Counter A popular method in shops is the vertical dispenser on the counter by the cash till. It can give details of special offers, new ranges etc.

Street You can always try handing out leaflets in the street to passers-by, but you should first enquire with the local Town Council if there are any bye-laws against doing this. The response rate is usually very low too.

Trade Shows Most people at trade shows are potential buyers and, depending on the particular Show, some may wish to make their purchasing decisions later. A leaflet is a particularly useful way to keep your product or service in front of them. Be careful you (or your staff) are not inadvertently handing out your leaflet to a competitor!

MONITORING

Just like any other advertisement, the success or otherwise of your leaflet should be quantified. See the item on Monitoring in the previous Chapter ∎

---

7 Common Errors When Producing A Leaflet

1. Being more concerned with the looks of a leaflet than its objectives.
2. Giving the printer poor artwork and expecting miracles.
3. Forgetting to emphasise the "unique selling proposition" of your business.
4. Omitting (or hiding) prices when this is critical to the reader's decision making.
5. Printing too many leaflets with details that date it quickly, requiring new ones to be printed, wasting old ones.
6. Giving insufficient thought to how the leaflet should best be distributed to reach the target readers.
7. Forgetting to monitor the response to the leaflet (it should be treated like any other advertisement).

Any business, and in particular a small or newish business, has to blow its trumpet very loudly indeed to be heard at all. Sadly few small businesses make use of the almost *free* trumpet-blowing publicity they can get by working closely with the Media.

The enterprising business can therefore get one step ahead by making full use of this excellent means of promotion. It will take up valuable time but done well it will represent some of the best marketing activity you can do. It is often referred to as "PR" (Public Relations).

By "media" we are referring to local newspapers, local radio, national and regional newspapers, Sunday papers, consumer magazines, trade press and television. Their readership/audiences cover all possible combinations of likely customers and will certainly include your target market.

THE MEDIA'S NEEDS
To get the most out of a relationship with the media requires primarily a basic understanding of their needs and requirements. The first point to note is these different publications and broadcast media consume news at an awesome rate. They have a perpetual requirement for new stories, especially good stories. Every business generates (or, as we shall see, contrives) at least several worthwhile stories every year. In general terms, what makes a good story is:

* Relevance to the media's readership/audience.
* Human Interest.
* Connection with other News stories.
* Timing.
* Entertainment value, eg something unusual, new or humorous.
* Availability of good photos.

Let us look at these aspects in relation to the different media.

Local Newspapers/Radio Here the need for "human interest" is vital, so telling them that you have just installed a new *Thingummy Zippy Mark 3* machine in the local City Chambers which will do all sorts of clever things is probably a non-starter of a news story. If however the installation of the new machine is likely to lead to the recruitment of new staff in an area of the country with high unemployment, then that would be interesting. If a new operator of the machine had to go somewhere interesting, especially if it was abroad, to receive training, then that would make an even better story. You can visualise the item's headline "Young Fred Flies To Florida" or whatever!

In fact, though the setting up of a new business, launching a new project, taking on more staff or changing premises *may* get some news coverage, the real trick is to look for a "connection". This could be historical. For instance if your project was related, however slightly, to the marine industry and you are doing something new some 25, 50 or whatever years after some well-known ship was launched, the connection might be "75 years after the S.S. Titanic was launched, a Belfast company today launches ....."

Alternatively the connection could be human interest and the same story might be "Grandson of yardworker who helped build the Titanic, today 75 years on, launches ...."

An entirely different connection is where you can link your own story with some other more major story that the local media are running. For instance, if a major continuing story has been the run-down of a large local factory then if one of the redundant workers sets up a new business employing several others from the factory then there is an obvious connection.

As for photographs, local newspapers will frequently use their own photographers as it is convenient for them, but it is always worthwhile sending good black & white prints if you have them.

National/Regional Newspapers
These tend, not surprisingly, to report matters of regional, national and international interest and importance. For a story to be suitable it would need

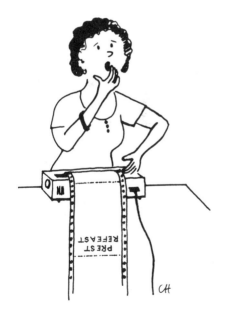

"Oh deer! My printerx gon wrung...."

to be of interest to a regional or national audience. Obviously you may have a story that is of interest to a regional paper but of less interest to a national one. Again, any connection with some major news story that the paper is already running increases the chances of inclusion.

Since the readership of these publications can be huge (even regional newspapers can have readerships in excess of a quarter of a million people) just a mention of your company or product, however small, can give your promotion quite a boost.

In such a situation in addition to sending your Press Release to selected national or regional papers you could also send it to the Press Association at 85 Fleet Street, London EC4P 4BE who provide a news service for virtually all newspapers, radio and TV.

Consumer Magazines   These have a different requirement for stories. Consumer magazines tend to be more specialist interest than news-orientated and have considerably less stories in an issue than any newspaper. Individual stories tend to be longer "features". A significant factor with these magazines is their use of colour and, in many cases, in contrast to newspapers, a much greater proportion of advertising. This creates many distractions for the reader. Within their specialist areas the consumer magazines have large readerships and considerable authority so editorial mention can be very beneficial (provided, of course, their comments are positive!).

These magazines are usually working on their feature articles several months ahead of the publication date. A phone call request to their advertising department will usually secure a "Features List". Should one of these features relate to your own business or line of business, then that is the connection you are looking for. You may then consider submitting a Press Release in ample time. If such a magazine closely follows your own target market you may also at some stage consider advertising in it as well. It would be worthwhile to make the effort to meet and speak to some of the editorial staff which could well pay dividends in the future.

Specialist Trade Press   These are magazines and newspapers which are distributed free or under subscription to a particular trade and rarely appear on the magazine racks of your local newsagent. Almost every trade has them and they act as useful disseminators of information within a trade. In fact many trade buyers base their purchasing decisions on, or are influenced by, what they read in the trade press. So if your customers are trade then editorial within the relevant trade magazines is indeed very useful to promoting your business.

Most trade magazines have 'News' sections and thrive on a diet of Press Releases. Whereas general consumer magazines are read essentially for pleasure, the reader of a trade publication has more serious motives. Thus a story that might be completely inappropriate for a consumer publication may be bread & butter to the relevant trade magazine — good examples being news of appointments, changes of business address, reports on Trade Shows and new products.

One important point to remember is that in some trade sectors a product may be unveiled to the trade many months before it is launched to consumers. In that case the product will require two Press Releases, one for the trade press and a second one several months later for the consumer press.

Television   Though many small businesses may think TV is 'too big' to be interested in them, this is not necessarily the case. A regional news programme or a series on a specialist topic relevant to your business could indeed be very interested in hearing from you.

In addition to the normal story requirements outlined above, it is important to understand that TV is first and foremost a visual medium. The story is unlikely to be shown unless it has a strong visual content — this normally entails movement and colour.

With the increasing deregulation of Television in the UK, opportunities for businesses to get exposure should increase. Television reaches 98% of homes (one third of homes actually have two or more TV sets!) and it is an astonishingly pervasive and persuasive medium.

SOME GENERAL POINTS
Talking To The Media   When talking to journalists from the local Press or radio, consumer magazines or trade publications you can normally talk fairly openly. The "off the record" or "don't quote me" type of remark should *never* be used unless you know the journalist concerned and have built up a degree of trust and confidence based on past reporting integrity.

If you are dealing with any sort of sensitive issue it is better to hand a prepared statement to the journalist so that he or she at least has your account of the situation. It is also advisable to keep a copy of the statement.

Some people have had bad experiences at the hands of the media, being misquoted or generally treated rather shabbily. Some publications, fortunately a minority, have a reputation for this. Contact with them therefore requires care, particularly if your business is suffering from problems which they can focus on, possibly distort and in any event cause you even greater problems. If in any doubt — do not say anything (however persistent they are) and contact your lawyer.

One Hurdle When dealing with some local papers or trade publications you may be confronted with the attitude that if you do not advertise with them it is unlikely you will get any editorial. If you are confronted with such blackmail you ought to consider choosing another publication and just keep up the pressure! Although these magazines or newspapers need all the advertising they can get and it is indeed proper for them to ask if you would like to advertise, this should not be a precondition for editorial.

No Story? Then Make One! When you do not have any particular story to tell but want to encourage some media attention a little ingenuity (a gimmick even) is required. This may sound a little cynical but it is equally useful for the media as it can provide (as it is intended) a light-hearted, amusing or unusual news item. It is often something visual and does require thought and planning and probably some expenditure. Typical aids to gain attention are — using personalities, trying to break records listed in the Guinness Book of Records and stunts.

Exclusive Stories All publications operate today in a very competitive environment and the opportunity of running an exclusive story, provided it is of sufficient quality and interest for their readers or audience, is attractive. If your story is of that quality try offering it to the best publication (from your point of view) and by explaining you will not offer it to anyone else if they use it, may increase its chances of being published.

Deadlines Journalists tend to be very busy people who have deadlines that hound them. They have to do background research, conduct interviews and write stories on several topics at the same time. Presenting your story in a professional manner helps them and significantly increases the chances of your item being published or broadcast. This is discussed further below.

No Guarantees Even if you submit a cracking good story to the right publication in a professional manner,

This photo which shows the event announcing BP's share price of £3.30 clearly demonstrates the details required to attract full media attention. The price was spectacularly unveiled across the front of BP's London HQ. Note the press corps on the roof bottom right and the band, podium and audience lower left. *(Photograph by British Petroleum)*.

Working With The Media — PR

and (most importantly) on time, there is no guarantee that the publication will use the story — for many good reasons of which lack of space is probably the most important. You should not be disappointed, but keep on trying, submitting other Press Releases in due course.

Also, assuming the Press Release has been sent to a number of media, hopefully at least one will use the story. Remember too that publications often re-write the information in their own words, probably abbreviating it greatly in the process.

Another aspect of Press Releases which must be clearly understood is that though you may wish it to be published or broadcast on a specific day or week, it may appear at any time, and possibly a long time after it is of much use to you.

If you have established some rapport with the editorial team there is no harm in asking at some later stage why the story was not used and this may provide some useful feedback. Equally, if the publication does use your story a short 'thank-you' note or phone-call would be very welcome!

PR People Big companies well know the value to be derived from working closely with the media — both printed and broadcast. They employ part-time (freelance) or full-time PR people. It is their job to feed the right media with lots of the right stories at the right time and to then gently cajole those media into using at least some of the stories.

As your business grows this is one activity you may consider contracting out to a professional PR person rather than trying to do it all by yourself. Until then the experience of doing it yourself will enable you to brief such a PR person properly and, equally, to understand what can and what cannot be achieved by PR alone.

SELECTING THE RIGHT MEDIA

With such a variety of media available, it is important to select those appropriate to your business, ie those media whose readership or audience matches as closely as possible your target market. This decision-making process is similar to that required when selecting which media to use for advertising — see the Chapter **Advertising — Why? Where? When?** The differences of course being that not every advertising medium carries editorial and with PR activity you can afford to spread your net a little wider.

If you are not familiar with any of the publications you think might be suitable, get a copy and see what subjects it covers and its style of reporting. You also need to know the deadlines by which time the publications must receive editorial information.

Compiling A Mailing List Since you will be sending out regular Press Releases, ie at least several times a year, and to a number of publications, it will save time in future to produce a mailing list.

Your main source of information about relevant publications, other than your own knowledge, will be BRAD. BRAD is a reference publication already described in the Chapter **Advertising-Why? Where? When?**

It is always better if you can address a Press Release to a named individual. You can find out names by a quick phone call to the relevant media (BRAD gives these phone numbers).

The relevant publications can then be entered onto any small PC-computer which has suitable software and a printer that can print out address labels. Alternatively you can type the names and addresses onto a master sheet which most High Street instant print shops can then photocopy onto self-adhesive address labels.

Quantity — v — Quality Some PR people seem to work on the *quantity* rather than *quality* principle and rush out huge volumes of any Press Release to all and sundry. This is a complete waste of effort for two reasons:
a) different publications have different needs (a simple example is that a trade magazine will publish a story that a consumer magazine would never consider as newsworthy) and b) a Press Release that has had excessively wide exposure becomes a little worn and of less value (particularly with the very competitive national newspapers all vying for something new and different). It is therefore much better to target your Press Releases, just as with any marketing mailshot.

PREPARING A PRESS RELEASE

A typical Press Release package may consist of one, two or even three parts which are:

1. The typed Press Release itself.
2. Photograph(s).
3. Sample(s).

THE PRESS RELEASE

A Press Release should be typed on a letterhead and clearly titled PRESS RELEASE. It should be double spaced which is easier to read quickly and allows the journalist to add comments or make changes. Other aspects (as reflected in the fictitious Press Release on the opposite page) are as follows.

PRESS RELEASE

NOT FOR PUBLICATION OR BROADCAST
BEFORE 2ND MAY 1990

SIMPLY PERFECT

12 Regent Crescent
Greenock
PA1 1ZZ
Tel: Greenock (0475) 242

LAUNCH OF NEW FASHION VENTURE IN GREENOCK

At a short ceremony in Greenock today, Miss Petunia Smart, well-known
actress, opened the new fashion boutique called SIMPLY PERFECT.

The shop, located at 12 Regent Crescent in Greenock, will stock ladies outerwear for
the mature successful woman. The range will include smart dresses, attractive skirts
with many co-ordinating blouses, dashing coats, head-turning hats and an extravaganza
of accessories.

Miss Joan Smith, 42, the proprietor of the new shop and a former teacher, said "At
present many ladies have to travel 18 miles to Paisley to look for smart outfits and
casual wear. I hope this new shop will meet their needs locally". Joan Smith has
visited the fashion houses in Paris, Milan and London to select her stock.

TV Personality, Miss Smart, who lives locally, said "I always need to dress well for
my TV appearances and I will certainly be making use of SIMPLY PERFECT. I spotted some
nice Italian blouses with floral prints".

The Director of the local Enterprise Agency, Mr Helpful, said "We are delighted to have
been able to assist Miss Smith with this venture. We helped her to prepare the necessary
Business Plan and provided other general start-up advice. This is our 100th new business
start-up that we have helped".

To introduce local ladies to the new stock, there will be a fashion show at a
Hotel on the 10th May. Tickets are available from the shop.

FOR FURTHER INFORMATION:

Miss Joan Smith
Tel: Greenock (0475) 242

PHOTOGRAPH attached

Proprietor: Joan Smith

Fictitious example

Shop Hours: Mon-Sat 0930-1730

Working With The Media — PR

Embargoes If you specifically do not want premature publicity you can use an embargo note on the top of the Press Release — this is a polite request to the recipient to not print anything on the story until the date (and sometimes a time too) as shown on the Press Release. But do realise with any embargo, that if you are launching some major project on a Tuesday, if you give the Press Release to daily newspapers and a Sunday newspaper, then the Sunday paper may be tempted to splash the story the Sunday before the event, because the following Sunday it will not be news anymore. Only use embargoes if it is essential.

Headline A good descriptive headline is essential allowing the first recipient to know if the Press Release applies to their department, (Sport, Business, Features, Travel, Women's Interest or whatever). Do not try to emulate a catchy newspaper headline style — leave that part to them!

Format The text of a Press Release consists of 3 parts:

1. The *Introduction* sets the scene and should be no longer than one short paragraph.
2. The *Main Body* describes the story, reflecting the comments given at the beginning of this Chapter. The media also tend to like quotes from relevant people so give them some! Finally, add people's ages, where possible. In terms of the actual text, it is important not to use superlatives or make suspect claims (eg the world's cheapest, largest, smallest etc... unless this is clearly the case).

Put the most important points first, because if space in a publication is tight (it usually is) most sub-editors delete from the bottom up. Also, the Press Release should never read like an advertisement selling your firm or its products/services — it should read like a News story.

3. A *Conclusion* is useful in most Press Releases, which could be a phrase such as "The whole range will be on show on Stand No X at the such-and-such Show".

Length One page should suffice, two only if it is a major story in which case the word 'MORE' should be typed at the foot of the first page and 'ENDS' at the end of the text on the second page. These little details ought to impress the professionals!

Other Details A well produced Press Release should also include several other pieces of information:

1. *Contact Name & Phone No.* so a journalist can phone for more information if required. Some people also include their home phone number.
2. If there is a *Photo* included this should be stated or alternatively, if you are only planning to send out a photo on request (why so mean?) then a comment such as "B/W Photos Are Available" could be added at the foot. (B/W = Black & White).
3. If there is no embargo date, then the *Date* when you have sent out the Press Release should be typed at the top or bottom.
4. Avoid jargon unless the Press Release is for a technical/trade publication, and spell out any abbreviations the first time you use them in any Press Release.

PHOTOGRAPH(S)

As to photographs, the following aspects need to be considered. First, is the publication you are sending the Press Release to a colour or mono magazine or newspaper? If most of its photos are in black & white, you need to send black & white photograph prints (usually not negatives) of a size about 5"x7" or 6"x8".

Second, these photos must be captioned, preferably by typing the caption on a piece of paper and then sticking the paper to the rear of the photo with tape, or by typing the caption on self-adhesive labels. NEVER write directly on the back of a photo using a ball-pen as the ink can come off easily when in contact with the front of another photo ruining the second photo. To remove ball-pen ink from a photo, try lightly dabbing the mark with a piece of cotton wool dipped in milk. This usually helps.

The caption should include your company name and address as photos can get accidentally separated from your Press Release.

Third, whenever photos are sent by post do ensure that they are in cardboard backed envelopes and marked "Photos Please Do Not Bend". The photos should be attached to the Press Release by a paper clip, never a staple or pin.

Finally, if the photos you are sending are rare, valuable or you need them returned, then send them by "Recorded Delivery" or "Registered Post" and ask for them back once the publication has finished with them. You might enclose a stamped addressed envelope if you are really keen to get the photos back.

SAMPLE(S)

Certain businesses may find it possible to send a sample or samples of their products with the Press Release. This can be very effective provided the sample is quite small, of relatively low value and it helps the recipient to understand the product. If sending an unrequested sample, it is not really acceptable to ask for it back as this is a nuisance for the recipient.

TIMING OF PRESS RELEASES

Although the media's own deadlines are paramount (because if your story arrives late it cannot be used!) there are other aspects of timing which need to be considered to get the most impact from your story:

Connections If you see a story running in a publication, or being broadcast, and your own story can be linked to it in some way then act before the mainstream story goes cold.

Thick & Thin Issues All publications have some thicker and some thinner issues in terms of content and pages. Some daily newspapers are thinner on Saturdays and Mondays, business publications are sometimes thinner in the summer months and so on. Obviously the chances of getting some exposure are higher when the publication is more hungry for news, though equally its readership may be less.

Crises One problem you cannot plan for is if there is a major regional or national crisis or disaster the day after you posted out your Press Releases, your story is likely to be dropped in favour of the other event. Try again later!

Time of Day Even the time of day is important if you are trying to catch a specific Radio or TV programme (eg local news), weekly newspapers, evening papers and so on.

Before or After? Should you send out a Press Release before an event or after? It obviously depends on the circumstances, but if in doubt, send out one before and a second (different) one after, thereby getting two opportunities for the media to use the story.

Follow Up An important activity is to follow up the Press Release by phoning the recipients to ensure they have received it, ask if they need any help and if they intend to use it.

---

5 Common Errors When Doing Press Releases

1. Writing very long (or boring) Releases.
2. Enclosing uncaptioned (or poor) photos.
3. Not making the company name clear.
4. Not dating a Press Release.
5. Sending a Press Release past a deadline — it's dead!

MONITORING

Carrying out PR work successfully takes time and some cash too. It therefore makes sense to monitor the response it is bringing, just like any other promotion you may be doing. It is too easy to be mesmerised by seeing your name in print, but what tangible benefit has that brought your business?

First you need to monitor which publications actually print your story and, where relevant, which broadcast media also use the story. This is more difficult than appears at first sight. If asking customers where they heard about your business, they are notoriously vague in this regard. It may need you to visit the Library and look through past issues of likely publications to see if they used the story.

Once you have established which media used your Press Release, you need to try to quantify the response it has brought your business. This may ultimately be little more than just a "good guess", but at least it will give you some idea of what your PR effort is doing for you.

PRESS CONFERENCES, PRESS DAYS, PHOTO CALLS

It is unlikely that a small business can command enough attention to justify a Press Conference but if the event was of regional/national importance and there was a VIP to make an important announcement then it might be possible.

On a smaller scale you can have "Press Days" when your premises/showroom is open to the Press who are invited and perhaps given some refreshments whilst being told about your company and its business. For this type of occasion you might give each journalist a "Press Pack" with a Press Release, photo(s) and general company information. It may contain any current leaflet or brochure, price list (if you want that public) and possibly background notes (even photos) of the partners/Directors and key staff. To make it look more professional the Press Pack should be presented in a folder. Remember to send copies of these Press Packs to any publication/radio etc that did not manage to attend.

A "Photo Call" is when there is something specific (and transient) to photograph, for instance there may be models wearing the latest fashions, or the opening of a new factory ■

Selling Techniques

The Customer Is King! But is this really so? Judging from the way some businesses treat their customers, he or she is barely a serf!

Many a sale has been lost by poor sales technique, yet the whole process of selling is obviously one of the key activities of any business.

Surprisingly, few staff outwith the sales team realise that their wages are derived directly from their customers. Too many appear to think their wage packets come from the company's coffers which keep full by magic!

This Chapter starts by looking at some of the general principles of selling, and then looks at the following specific selling situations:

1. Selling Face-to-Face (non-retail).
2. Retailing.
3. Telephone Sales.
4. Selling From An Exhibition Stand.

But first some buzz words. Professional salespeople refer to "target customers" (who are all those people who might buy, ie the total likely market), "prospects" (who are those prospective customers who *may* buy); "customers" (who are prospects who have become buyers) and "key accounts" (who are the large buyers).

Why Do People Buy Anything?
People as individuals (or acting for the companies or organisations for whom they work) make purchasing decisions for only two reasons: a) to meet an essential need or b) to meet a non-essential need, ie a desire.

Essential Needs For individuals, such needs might include basic foods, gas or electricity while for companies they might include raw materials. One *has* to make the purchasing decision and the only variables are: a) who to buy from and b) what quantity to buy. In practice there might also be an element of choice. Since the customer is almost forced to make a purchasing decision the selling technique is primarily concerned with encouraging him or her to choose your business rather than the competition.

Non-Essential Needs In contrast, here the potential customer need not buy at all, so your efforts are to attract his or her interest and then to work on closing the sale. Even essential items such as clothing need to be treated more in terms of a non-essential purchase since the choice is so vast and the potential customer might even decide simply not to buy any new clothes at all!

Hence catering for non-essential needs involves a definite two-stage selling process.

One particular type of non-essential purchasing is when a customer buys on impulse. This is reflected particularly in the retail sector with store layouts and point-of-sale items near the cash till.

Sell The Benefits!
There is an old saying that "customers buy benefits, not features". What this means is best illustrated by an example. Electronic contact-less ignition may be a *feature* of some new cars, but the purchaser is more interested in the *benefits* this brings, such as easy starting, keeping in-tune longer and so on. In fact many drivers will not even know (or care about) what contact-less ignition is — all they will know is that their car starts and runs with less trouble.

A common fault with both service and manufacturing businesses is they get so carried away with all the clever bits of their business, they may forget the customer is only interested in what benefit those clever bits may bring.

However, it is the unique features of your business which give you a competitive edge so the selling line should be something like... "the benefit to you is .... because of (the feature)". No benefit = no interest = no sale!

Enthusiasm Is Infectious
All successful salespeople are enthusiasts or at least they are able to appear to be enthusiasts when they are trying to sell something. They will be enthusiastic about what they have to sell, their company, their life and will also be enthusiastic about the customer's business. There is no quicker way to kill off a potential buyer's interest than being unenthusiastic. In some contexts such as retailing or at an Exhibition, it may require some effort to maintain this enthusiasm over a long day.

Trade Buyer or Consumer
There are significant differences between trade buyers and consumers (ie the general public). The fact that the same person appears to behave quite differently when spending firm's money to when spending their own is a revealing point about human nature.

Consumers Once a consumer's basic needs of food, shelter and clothing are met, much more complex reasons for buying things come into play. Thus purchasing decisions have more to do with portraying social or financial success than the intrinsic usefulness of whatever is bought; purchasing decisions may also relate to hobbies, sports or pastimes; also purchasing decisions may reflect prestige and, to a certain extent, following the herd. These desires are the result of our up-bringing and experiences but are very much shaped by the media and the influence of friends and family. They play a crucial role in terms of non-essential purchasing behaviour.

The cash available to meet a consumer's purchasing wishes is often limited, or requires credit facilities.

Consumers also tend to show great concern about relatively small sums of money, sometimes choosing a particular product or service almost *solely* because of price.

Trade Buyers Their needs differ in some marked respects. First and foremost their primary concern is that whatever they buy must do its job, be delivered or done on time and give them the least *problems*. The quality of the product or service is usually more important than the price. That is not to say that price is irrelevant but simply that it often has a lower priority, provided it is within the budget allocated. In contrast to an individual consumer the buying power of even a small business is considerably greater but still, credit terms will normally be requested and there is always the risk of a business defaulting on payment. Another characteristic of selling to certain trade buyers is you may be involved in competitive tendering.

All buyers (trade or consumer) like to be made to feel they are important (they are!) and they like to feel that they have either secured a good deal or at least a fair deal.

CUSTOMER CARE

If you are really genuinely concerned about your customers, some of this will come naturally anyway, but a few ideas to improve customer care are as follows:

1. Listen to them. In this way their needs can be found (and met) and you will get good feed-back in terms of what they think of whatever you are already supplying. Future opportunities may also reveal themselves.
2. Think about them. Even worry on their behalf! Remember they may have their own problems too.
3. Pay attention to detail, eg don't leave customers "hanging on a phone" or waiting at your Reception.
4. Keep in touch. People like to feel that you care about them and any contact from you which is not specifically to sell them something is usually much appreciated.
5. Think of customers as individuals when sending out mailshots, designing adverts or thinking of your shop window display. Don't think of your customers *en masse*, but rather as individual people.

6. Generate 'Customer Loyalty'. This is not easily achieved, particularly when dealing with the general public. It has to be built up over a period of time and worked on. You are establishing a rapport, a relationship, and this can be of crucial importance if you are confronted with an aggressive competitor or your business goes through a sticky patch.
7. Apologise if an error is made, as anyone can make a mistake. Many big businesses are not good at apologising, so it gives small businesses a chance to demonstrate they are more 'human'. However, if there is any possibility of someone claiming damages because of an alleged error you have made, get legal advice before replying.
8. Treat rude customers politely. Try to resist the temptation to tell them bluntly what you think of them. Being polite but firm is not only good manners but can pay future dividends as they sometimes become loyal customers!

Customer Records Particularly with trade buyers, you should keep a detailed record of your customers and potential customers. This can consist of a card index system with one card per customer, as illustrated below. These lined cards and their boxes are available in a range of sizes from most stationers. Each card should have the customer's full name and address, with contact name(s) and job titles.

WORTHLESS PRODUCTS LTD
Unit 3, Industrial Estate   Gen Mgr: A McSwindle
Birmingham B1 1ZZ   Secretary: Claire
Tel: 021-123 456
Fax: 021-123 000   Keen golfer!

22.5.90	Sent leaflet with covering letter.
31.5.90	Phoned. McS in meeting – try tomorrow.
1.6.90	Phoned. Spoke to McS – visit 13/6 at 2pm.
13.6.90	Visited. See notes on file. Left sample of mesh.
14.6.90	Sent quote for 4 windows – mesh £639.
	* Remember to phone on 19/6 to follow-up quote.

FICTITIOUS EXAMPLE OF A CUSTOMER RECORD CARD

Selling Techniques

You can then record details every time contact is made by phone or in person. The card might also record any special ordering details relating to that customer. Though it takes time and effort to complete these cards and keep them up-to-date, as any seasoned salesperson would agree, they are invaluable.

Time & Effort per Customer How much time and effort you should expend on individual customers can be a problem. Sometimes small customers take up a disproportionate amount of your time (in relation to the value of their business) but they might be loyal, use your company regularly and may pay their bills quickly. Other small customers might simply be difficult to deal with and poor payers too! Large customers can equally be good or bad to deal with. A point to watch is that you should never be dazzled by big orders from one or two major buyers to the extent that you ignore your smaller customers. Large orders tend to involve: a) lower margins; b) longer credit; c) greater dependence and d) any failure to pay might prove fatal to your own business. In the meantime your smaller customers may have found alternative and more sympathetic suppliers.

We now consider typical selling situations.

FACE TO FACE SELLING

Selling face-to-face can occur when dealing with a trade customer or in a door-to-door sales situation. It could be "cold calling", ie you have no appointment, or you may have an appointment as a result of your advertising or through sending out a mailshot.

Not surprisingly, most salespeople do not like cold calling. It is hard work, takes a lot of time, has a low success rate and you can be confronted with some pretty rude responses. (Regrettably some businesses who actively sell their own products or services can be quite rude when anyone else tries to sell them something!).

For a small business with its limited manpower, it should ensure that the people being visited are likely prospects. A little research beforehand will reduce the number of wasted visits. If cold-calling is essential then you should at least first "soften up the target" with an advance mailshot and/or advertising.

In any event, to ensure as successful an outcome as possible, preparation before you set out is essential:

Dress If you have not met the contact before, they will assess you and your company in a matter of moments on the basis of your appearance and dress. Smartness, neatness and a style of clothing appropriate to the situation is called for — most business requires a fairly conservative style of dress.

Sales Material This is a key element in face-to-face selling. It may consist of your business card, sample(s), price list, brochures, Customer Record Card, order form and possibly a calculator if you need to produce an on the spot estimate or quotation. A pen and paper is obviously required too.

Sales material should be known backwards. It is not good enough to have to search through a brochure every time a question is asked.

If you do not have a good brochure and it is not possible to carry samples due to their size, a very effective sales tool is a photo album with clear pockets (such as the Rexel Nyrex Slimview Display Books) into which you slip an A4 piece of blank paper onto which are fixed photos with a typed description. The photos can illustrate your premises and staff (to give more credibility to your operation), photos of your products and where possible the product (or service) in use by other customers to gain further credibility. People all love to look at *good* photos and it should help your sales pitch. The album can also contain letters of commendation (testimonials), certificates of technical competence, cuttings from newspapers, membership of trade association diplomas and so on. Of course you need not show every page to every customer.

If as is likely in this type of selling you are having to walk or travel, a route map is obviously another essential item and any route should be planned carefully in advance to make the most of your time.

Handling The Interview
Here are some tips for the actual sales interview:

1. First, there is no need to be nervous as people enjoy chatting to nice people and you have an excellent product (or service) to sell.
2. Don't run up stairs or along corridors if you are a little late. It will soon make you out of breath which if you are slightly nervous will make you breathe heavily.
3. If you are going to be late for an appointment, if possible phone and let them know you are running late.
4. On meeting the "prospect", give a firm handshake and hand over your business card if you have not met before.
5. In a business context, if you are not

sure of the prospect's full name and job title, ask for his or her business card.

6. Our business etiquette usually requires an exchange of pleasantries to break the ice before getting down to business. It is useful to have something sensible and non-contentious to talk about for a few minutes. Old favourites are to talk about the weather, your journey, the news headlines and the latest sports results.

7. Then either the prospect will give an indication that he or she wants to talk business (or if not you can just launch off yourself). Initially you will have to start off talking. It is worthwhile having an idea of what you are going to say, ie a little pre-planned speech which explains very quickly what you have to offer and promises some exciting benefits for the listener. You only have a minute or two to catch the prospect's interest. However do not get into the rigid habit of using your set piece speech every time — listen to and observe the prospect's reactions and react to them.

8. Hopefully your introductory speech will have interested the prospect enough for him or her to ask some questions or agree to see your catalogue/samples. If possible try to demonstrate something, as this can be both appealing and persuasive.

At this stage you should listen carefully to find out their *needs* as this allows you to fine-tune the next part of your presentation to match those needs, explaining how your product or service can do that.

9. As the interview develops, try asking more open questions, which will not only show your interest in the prospect and their company, but will help you to learn more too. You may learn about other possible opportunities which can be investigated or developed later.

10. If the prospect raises objections, this is healthy and the objections should be listened to carefully. It may even help you to jot down what is said so that you can overcome these objections one at a time without missing any.

11. Close the sale (see below), get the buyer to sign a copy of the order form and leave them a duplicate copy of the order which should always include the agreed price. Alternatively, your business might be one where you need to go away and then send a written quotation.

12. Once the sale is over, don't hang around. The customer will appreciate you leaving promptly (they have their own work to do). If no sale is made but there is a possibility of a sale in the future, ensure you keep the door open by leaving your card, any relevant brochure (but don't sink the poor prospect under a ton of paper) and, where appropriate, make a tentative appointment for the future.

NB: The Consumer Protection (Cancellation of contracts concluded away from Business Premises) Regulations 1987 provide for a 7-day cooling-off period during which agreements covered by these Regulations can be cancelled by the consumer. If involved in selling away from business premises, eg in people's homes, then get a leaflet on this from your local Trading Standards Officer.

Hard Sell-v-Soft Sell Salespeople fall into two camps — some do a "hard sell", while others prefer to adopt a "soft sell" approach. Characteristics of the hard sell brigade tend to include fast talking, elaborate and possibly

On meeting the prospect give a firm handshake. (But not too firm!)

exaggerated claims, continual reference to other buyers (so you feel you are missing out if you do not buy) and insistence that you order now. In general you feel under considerable pressure with such a salesperson and resent the method — not to be encouraged if further sales are hoped for.

The soft sell approach in contrast lets the customer get a word in edgeways, queries and objections are dealt with and there is much less feeling of being under pressure to buy and buy now.

Although none of us like to be on the receiving end of a hard sell (and in fact some people totally reject it) there is no doubt it can be very successful in certain specific situations, especially

Selling Techniques

when dealing with relatively un-sophisticated buyers.

Techniques For Closing The Sale
You must learn to be able to sense when a prospect is ready to buy.

1. He or she may start to ask detailed questions, talk about methods of payment or enquire about delivery. Then you can close the sale by, for instance, taking out your order book (very visibly) and asking something like "so, how many .... do you want in your first order?" or "on what date would you like your first order delivered?" (and then you can discuss quantities).
2. Another technique is to completely by-pass the Yes/No decision of the customer and jump to asking if the customer would like this option or that, concluding by writing out an order in the usual way.
3. If the customer is unsure because he or she needs a colleague's/boss's opinion, ask that colleague/boss to join your discussions or arrange to come back and see them all (ie try not to let them decide in your absence!).
4. If the customer says he or she needs to "think it over" before deciding, then leave something like your personal catalogue (suitably marked "ONLY COPY") or some samples which you arrange to collect the next day (or day after — don't let it cool too far). This tactic allows you to see the customer face-to-face again which gives you a second opportunity to close the sale and it is much more difficult for the customer to turn you down in person, than over a phone.
5. Very often you can detect a customer is interested but is wavering. The key to closing the sale is to find out what is

Excellent use of a Shop Window promoting a new shop

causing them to be uncertain, so ask some questions — Is it the price? Colour? or whatever. Only then can you overcome the objections and move on to close the sale.
6. Overcoming the Price Barrier. Another common situation is the customer wants to buy but is unsure they can afford it. If this is the only sticking point you should be able to close the sale by having already prepared several different payment options or by offering a straightforward incentive discount, provided they decide there and then.
7. Before you close the sale, an experienced buyer may suddenly try to force a concession, such as a discount or early delivery or "throwing in" something (eg a free installation) which is normally charged extra. When faced with that try to get something in return, so if a discount was requested

you might agree provided the usual credit period was set aside and the bill was paid in full immediately.
8. Sometimes you may feel you are having a successful sales interview but you have not detected any buying signals and the meeting is beginning to drag. In such a situation you have to remember the purpose of the meeting is for you to sell something. You should buck up the courage to ask the direct question, something like "Well, I've shown you our complete range and it does seem the X or Y will suit your needs, so which would you like to order?"

RETAILING

Small independent shops fall into two distinct categories — "convenience shops" such as a newsagent, and

Selling Techniques

"specialist shops" such as a fashion boutique. In a convenience shop the customer tends to make most of his or her purchasing decisions before they enter and in a specialist shop the customer tends to make his or her decision after they enter. That is a simplification but it emphasises the differences in selling technique.

In the former case there is little 'selling' as you are primarily responding to the customer's requests, though selling can still play a part by getting the customer to buy additional purchases. For instance, a customer may enter a newsagents asking for his or her regular motoring magazine and the alert shop assistant might say "Have you seen this new annual survey of the best European cars?" and thereby encourage an extra sale.

Let us concentrate on the specialist shops where more active selling is required. Here are some suggestions:
1. Always acknowledge the presence of a customer very soon after they enter the shop, by a nod, smile and possibly a "Hello" or "Good Morning" even if you are already dealing with another customer. This makes them feel more at home on unfamiliar territory (especially if they have not visited the shop before) and it also tends to 'hold' them until you are free to help them.
2. Let the customer browse for a few moments and then approach them. The ideal moment is when they stop to examine or touch something. Do not say "Can I help you?" as you will get the universal reply "No, I'm just looking!" which stops your sales pitch dead in its tracks. Instead, use a question more related to the situation. For instance, if a lady is looking at blouses, you might ask "Is the blouse to match a particular skirt?..what colour?..day wear or evening

wear?...". Near Christmas you might ask "Is it a Christmas present you are looking for?". The key point with these questions is they allow you to start a conversation, which has several advantages: a) it stops the customer rushing around the shop and then disappearing out the door, b) it allows you to find out what the customer needs, c) it allows you to offer your products to match those needs and d) the customer will think you are being helpful. On the other hand, being too pushy can lose sales.
3. Where practical, encourage the shopper to handle the goods. This helps to create a 'bond' between the customer and the article for sale.
4. A retailer in a specialist shop will often be regarded by the shopper as an 'expert' so you do need to know your subject. Opinions, though, should be voiced, wherever possible, after you know your customer's views.
5. A key element of any retailing is the "add-on sale", ie it is the shoe polish when you buy a pair of shoes; the gift wrapping (when its not free) when you are buying a gift, and so on. Once a customer is in a buying mood, they are open to being shown and sold additional items, especially if they are related to the first purchase.
6. Just like the salesperson conducting a face-to-face interview, you need to know all the stock and options so that if a customer picks up one item but expresses a preference for a slightly different item, you immediately know what you have in stock, including any suitable alternatives.
7. With a small specialist shop, it is very off-putting for a customer to be alone with an assistant who is doing nothing. The customer will feel "watched". The assistant should therefore appear to be

busy, but without ignoring the customer. Soft background music can be useful too.
8. As in all selling, you need to be aware of when a customer is ready to buy and some of the comments above in 'Techniques For Closing The Sale' are appropriate.

The Shop Window This is a crucial factor especially in selling from a specialist shop. The window is the magnet that draws people in (very often on an impulse). It should be bright (actually lit up with lots of lights), attractive and articles on display should be clearly priced.

The window should be changed weekly or fortnightly and it should have a theme such as a subject or a common colour. For ideas, look at the windows of the big department stores (who all have full-time professional window dressers) and take notes to use for your own shop.

Dressing a window successfully can make a big improvement to sales, but is not easy to do. It may take several attempts before you get the shape, props, colours, and range of products right. If really stuck, there are freelance window dressers you can use.

Sales Material You should have showcards and posters or stickers which are produced by the suppliers of the stock you are carrying. They may also provide leaflets. These are all helpful as they brighten up a shop and, more importantly, show off the products to their best. They may also reflect a national advertising campaign theme, which customers have seen.

Layout The shop layout is important to assist your selling and should be

Selling Techniques

discussed with shopfitters. In particular, thought should be given to:

a) *Circulation* How are people to enter, move around, approach the cash desk and then leave. There should be a natural "route" which takes them round all, or most of, the shop.

b) *Display* Are items displayed at their best? The scan of most people's eyes is very limited as they browse in a shop — from about 12″ above eye height down to about 2′ above the floor, and anything above eye height will only be seen if standing away from the display. Then can people reach items easily? Prominence should be given to best sellers and the more expensive items should not be close to the door as it will give an initial impression of the shop being expensive and there is also the problem of shop-lifting. Stock should be rotated regularly.

c) *Signs* Though a retailer may know his or her stock very well, it can be very confusing for a new customer who has just entered the shop, so some attempt to group similar products together and use signs will help.

d) *Security* Shop-lifting is a major problem for retailers and the layout of the shop can either make it easier or more difficult for shop-lifters. The layout should not have any blind spots, ie staff should be able to see every part of the shop (perhaps with the use of mirrors). Small high value items are particularly vulnerable as is any stock positioned near the doorway.

e) *Point-of-Sale* These displays are very important (as seen particularly in supermarkets) where low-price, small, impulse-buy, popular goods can be displayed (and sold) to good effect.

General If you want to understand any of these points on Layout more clearly, you only have to visit a few of the better-known High Street stores to see how professionals tackle these aspects and to gain lots of ideas.

TELEPHONE SALES

Sometimes abbreviated to "Telesales", the telephone is a most useful tool, however to use it effectively requires skill and practice.

Selling by phone is a technique which is of particular use to the small business with limited manpower and where the proprietor(s) often has to do the sales work in addition to running the rest of the business.

The main uses of the phone in this context are:

a) Cold calling prospects.
b) As a follow up to a sales letter, either to make an appointment or secure a sale.
c) In response to someone contacting your business wanting more information or to place an order.

The main advantages of selling by phone are: a) you can contact would-be customers from your own desk, or with the use of a mobile phone or car phone whilst travelling around; b) a large number of people can be contacted in a relatively short time and c) with a bit of persistence you can usually get through to the decision maker.

Its main disadvantages are: a) you cannot show your product or other sales material to the customer and b) you cannot see their facial reactions. In addition, since most telesales calls are cold calling, one gets a fair amount of negative reaction, even rudeness, however polite you may be.

If you are making unsolicited telephone approaches to consumers, you should ensure that the calls comply with the Office of Fair Trading Guidelines, which can be found printed in the British Telecom Phone Books.

Preparation As with any sales work, preparation is essential so you must know who you are calling and what you are trying to achieve with the call. This is where the Customer Record Cards mentioned earlier in this Chapter become invaluable.

Handling The Conversation As there is no visual contact it is important in your opening statement to identify yourself and your company. This opening statement should be pre-written and rehearsed. So should your fact-finding questions and your sales message, but not rehearsed to the point of sounding like a tape recording! Several other hints are as follows:

* Try to keep a smile on your face (it shows in your voice).
* Keep your product/sales information in front of you as it will help you to remember details and to describe things.
* Remember the customer will be thinking "What's in this for me?", and since you have interrupted whatever they were doing, they may be impatient to get back to that.
* Close the sale, or where appropriate, arrange an appointment to see them.
* Since there is nothing in writing as yet, always summarise what has been agreed (then perhaps confirm it in writing by letter, fax or telex).
* A nice touch is to pause then put your phone down *after* the other person.
* Record the call on your Customer Record Card or use an A-Z lined notebook as a Sales Enquiry Book. This could list all the information.

To save time, with a little practice, this record keeping can be done while you are still on the phone. To remind you which customers you need to call back, place their Customer Record Cards on their ends so they stand up.

EXHIBITIONS

Participating in Exhibitions, Consumer Shows and Trade Shows has become an increasingly important facet of business life. (In this section we use the words Exhibition and Show interchangeably). For non-retail businesses they provide regional, national or even international exposure and contacts which are vital and might otherwise be very difficult to make. However, many new participants in Exhibitions are often disappointed with the results of their initial showings. This is mainly due to two factors, which are inexperience and unrealistically high expectations. (It might also be, one should add, their product or service is not of sufficient interest to potential buyers).

Exhibiting at any Show requires a great deal of preparation, an adequate budget and hard work before, during and afterwards to make the most of it. The decision to participate should not be made hastily with inadequate resources allocated to the task.

Where To Exhibit? You may already be familiar with the various Shows relevant to your own trade. Listed right is a brief selection to indicate that there are Shows for almost every trade sector imaginable. If in doubt ask other people in your trade. In addition to these large shows there are the various Agricultural Shows and many minor Exhibitions which are held around the country.

Even a very small business should

A SMALL SELECTION OF UK TRADE & PUBLIC SHOWS

SHOW	LOCATION	ORGANISERS
Amusement Trades Exhib	Earls Court, London	Amusement Trades, 071-713 0302
AUTOTECH[2] (Auto Technology)	NEC, Birmingham	Centre Exhibitions, 021-780 4141
Boat, Caravan & Leisure Show	NEC, Birmingham	B'ham Post & Mail, 021-236 3366
British Craft Trade Fair	Harrogate	Blenheim Events, 081-742 2828
British Footwear Fair	NEC, Birmingham	Blenheim Premier, 071-323 3302
British Int'l Toy & Hobby Fair	Olympia, London	British Toy & Hobby, 071-701 7127
Business Computing	Earls Court, London	Montbuild, 071-486 1951
EXSL (Exhib of Sports & Leisure)	NEC, Birmingham	Montbuild, 071-486 1951
Farnborough[2] (Aircraft & Eqpt)	Farnborough	Soc'y Brit Aero Cos, 071-839 3231
Fast Food Fair	Brighton	Reed Exhibitions, 081-948 9800
Harrogate Gift Fair	Harrogate	Blenheim Events, 081-742 2828
Harrogate Int'l Toy Fair	Harrogate	Harrogate Toy Fair, 071-226 6653
IFE[2] (Food & Drink Exhib)	Earls Court, London	Interbuild Exhibs, 071-486 1951
IFSEC (Fire & Security Exhib)	NEC, Birmingham	Blenheim Events, 081-742 2828
INTERBUILD[2] (Building & Construction)	NEC, Birmingham	Building Trades Exhib, 071-486 1951
Interior Design Int'l	Olympia, London	ID Exhibitions, 071-486 1951
Int'l Spring & Autumn Fairs	NEC, Birmingham	Trade Promtn Services, 081-855 9201
Int'l Watch, Jewellery & Silver Trades	Earls Court, London	Reed Exhibitions, 081-948 9800
IPEX[5] (Printing Industry)	NEC, Birmingham	Reed Exhibitions, 021-705 6707
London Int'l Boat Show	Earls Court, London	Nat Boat Shows, 0784 473377
London Int'l Book Fair	Olympia, London	Reed Exhibitions, 081-948 9800
London Interseason (Clothing)	B.D.C., London	Barker Brown, 071-637 3313
London Motor Show[2]	Earls Court, London	Philbeach Events, 071-370 8203
Motor Show[2]	NEC, Birmingham	SMMT, 071-235 7000
NEPCON (Electronic prodn eqpt)	NEC, Birmingham	Reed Exhibitions, 081-948 9800
Offshore Europe[2]	Aberdeen	Spearhead Exhibs, 081-549 5831
PPLE[2] (Professional Photo Lab Expo)	Wembley, London	Assoc of Photo Labs, 071-405 2762
Premier (Clothing)	NEC, Birmingham	Blenheim Premier, 071-323 3302
RoSPA (Safety & Health)	NEC, Birmingham	Centre Exhibitions, 021-780 4141
Salon Int'l (Hairdressing products)	Wembley, London	First Event, 071-252 7459
SCOTBUILD[2] (Building & Construction)	SECC, Glasgow	S.I.T.E., 031-556 5152
Scottish Engineering[2]	SECC, Glasgow	S.I.T.E., 031-556 5152
Southampton Int'l Boat Show	Southampton	So'ton Int'l Boat Show, 0703 737311
Stitches (Needlework etc)	NEC, Birmingham	Int'l Craft & Hobby, 0425 272711
World of Hospitality[2] (Hotel & Catering)	Earls Court, London	Reed Exhibitions, 081-948 9800
World Travel Market	Earls Court, London	Reed Exhibitions, 081-948 9800

Note 1. A small number beside the Show name (eg IFE[2]) indicates the Show is only held every 2 years.

Note 2. There is currently great turbulence in the exhibition industry with many Shows appearing, disappearing or being re-named.

Selling Techniques

consider participating in major Shows, but before deciding you should make yourself familiar with the Exhibition by going to it at least once as a visitor. Also, contact the organisers for details of Stand availability, costs and (just like placing an advertisement) details of just who has visited the previous Shows. The better national Shows are now very organised in this respect and can provide very specific visitor data.

Exhibition space is usually offered as either a bare site or a "basic" (also called a "shell") Stand which usually comprises carpet, walls and a name board. Exhibitions these days are quite sophisticated and there is nothing worse than an amateur looking stand sitting amongst those that have been professionally done so a basic or "shell" Stand is worthwhile.

The best Shows have their Stand space booked many months in advance, with exhibitors booking the next Show (which may be one or even two years away) while attending the previous one. This makes it difficult for the first-time exhibitor to break in, but it does mean that once a decision has been made to participate in a Show, you should immediately apply for stand space.

What Will It Cost? Costs for Stands are usually quoted in terms of £ per square metre but only certain sizes will be available, eg 2 x 3 metres or whatever. Choose the smallest stand space necessary to display your products. Having a larger stand does not generate more passing traffic. Note that often essential items such as lighting, 13Amp electric sockets, phone points and chairs are often quoted extra (and can be disproportionately expensive).

While working out the cost of participating in any Exhibition, you also need to remember the *real* cost should include accommodation (if the Show is not local), travel, carriage of exhibits, extra brochures you need printing, and so on. There may be other costs too such as the cost of building your own display, Insurance (remember to talk to your Insurers) and promotion. There is also the less quantifiable cost of being away from your normal work-place and normal sales activity for a period of days, perhaps as long as a week.

What Can Be Achieved? Just what can a small business achieve from participating in a Show, which can be both an expensive and time-consuming activity?

For a Trade Show, ie one where the majority of visitors are trade buyers, an initial objective is usually to "write some business" during the Show itself (ie actually take some orders) but the main objective is to meet new potential customers and, wherever possible, to arrange to see them after the Show. It is this follow up activity which is so vital. A new exhibitor may use the Show to find Agents or Reps (by putting up a small sign in the Stand to that effect). A Trade Show also lets you see existing customers, some of whom you may not have seen for some time. A small business really cannot afford to attend a Show simply to "show the flag". Typically the first appearance at a Trade Show will not produce dramatic results as trade buyers tend to be conservative, and stick to familiar suppliers, but by the second and third appearance you should be able to justify the costs of attending by the amount of business you are doing both at the Show and immediately after by following up the contacts made.

For a Consumer Show, what you can achieve depends on what you are selling. If you are selling relatively expensive products or services (eg cars, boats, caravans, conservatories etc) then you may take some orders at the Show but rather like the Trade Show the main business is likely to come from following up the enquiries made during the Show. In contrast, if you are selling a relatively cheap item, then you would be more likely to calculate the success of the Show simply by the amount of sales made there and then. This is then akin to retailing and the sales techniques of retailing apply.

An important long-term benefit of participating in any type of Show is it gives exposure to your name and what you do. So even if a person does not buy anything now, the next time they see your business name, it will help that important reinforcement which overcomes buyer resistance.

Stand Design Decide how the Stand is to be designed and if it requires props to be built and other visual aids (eg poster-size photos) made. Although it may sound obvious, a surprising number of Stands do not indicate clearly to a passer-by just *what* they are selling. If this is the first time you have designed a stand, either get professional advice or set aside time to look at other people's stands at previous exhibitions to see what attracts you. The design must catch a passer-by's attention and encourage them onto the stand. This is not easy as there is a tendency to walk past. Eye-catchers include light, movement, activity and emphasising things that are NEW. All signs should be done professionally.

Preparation Typically preparations should also include the following:

a) read the Rules & Regulations supplied by the organisers. Ensure fire prevention and safety requirements are met; b) decide who is going to man the stand (it is very tiring indeed to man a stand for long stretches so it needs a shift system, with usually more than one person on the stand for most periods); c) arrange accommodation close to the Exhibition; d) decide what literature is required in terms of hand-outs (brochures, price-lists) and, possibly, free samples. If things need printing this all takes time; e) obtain entry and car park passes for all your staff from the organisers; f) ensure there is adequate publicity given to ensure the maximum number of people visit the Show and, more importantly, your Stand. For trade shows this is best done by editorial and advertising in the relevant trade press, and for certain Shows, an advert in the Show Catalogue. In addition for trade shows all your customers and potential customers should receive a printed invitation from yourselves to visit the Show (most organisers can supply pre-printed invitation cards for you). For consumer shows you should again try to get as much publicity as possible in the relevant consumer press, and you may choose to advertise as well.

A brief plan of action should be drawn up, discussed with your partners, Directors and staff (especially those on the sales side) well in advance of the show and, most importantly, your objectives should be agreed upon and responsibilities allocated.

Staff Training Selling from a Stand is an unique experience which requires an understanding and training as with any other aspect of business. Simply knowing your business, trying hard and meaning well may not be good enough. Selling at an Exhibition incorporates aspects of retailing together with those of face-to-face selling. But the environment is unusual − the bright lights, music (or just noise), flashy displays, hospitality and hype all give a sense of unreality. It is also very fatiguing manning a Stand for several days.

The Exhibition Itself The day finally arrives and you find yourself on the Stand, perhaps nervously hoping buyers will come by and stop.

The first thing to overcome is the resistance people may feel about walking on to a small Stand. (The same problem faces small boutiques). The resistance is maximum when there is only one person on the stand and they are either "guarding" it (by standing in the middle like a sentry), or sitting in the middle passing the time reading (!). Resistance is also created by a Stand which has a layout which makes someone feel they are going to be trapped. You should look welcoming (not bored), not be so busy talking to each other that to venture onto the Stand feels like an intrusion, and yet you should appear to be busy (even if this is fictitious make-work). Keeping to the sides of the Stand is better than in the middle (not easy with a very small Stand). With really tiny stands, it is not possible to have more than one person manning it and the only thing you can do is to stand outside the Stand (and far enough away so that you do not seem to be hovering guarding it). This is a tricky compromise.

When someone comes onto the Stand (there should be plenty of things for them to see/inspect/touch) then, just like a retailer, you leave them for a few moments until they stop at something then you approach and ask a question relevant to the object/photo or whatever they are looking at. The straight "Can I help you?" question should be avoided. By listening you can find out the visitor's needs.

Some Trade Shows are organised enough to provide name tags which are very helpful as you can then see who you are dealing with, otherwise you should ask (it may be a competitor checking you out!).

The sales interview should then proceed along the lines already covered in this Chapter.

Whenever handing out a brochure, try to get the name/address of the prospect so you can follow it up later.

Security You should not forget about security. Your Stand is vulnerable to trade competitors, so customer lists and completed Order Forms should be guarded and new designs of equipment should not be left unattended.

Theft is also a problem at many Shows, either during the Show or over-night.

Exhibition Over When the last visitor leaves it is time to dismantle the Stand. The temptation to do this earlier should be resisted as you can often make a good contact in the closing minutes of a Show. Care should be taken when packing exhibits and display boards as they will certainly be required again.

Then comes the important follow up stage, contacting all those people who came onto your Stand ∎

Promoting Sales

There are almost as many other ways of promoting sales as there are business ideas. Although they are often cheaper than conventional advertising, they still cost money and in particular, time. One must therefore continually question their value and likely return.

Much of the promotional activity carried out by large corporations could, if measured, never be justified on commercial grounds alone and a small business cannot indulge itself to the same extent. There must therefore always be a sensible profit motive for carrying out any particular promotion and, as always, the promotion must be part of your overall marketing plan — fitting in with advertising, PR work and sales efforts.

It is important that any promotional work takes into account your own sales distribution method, ie you need to direct your promotion at that part of the distribution network where the key buying decisions are made, which may not always be obvious. For instance a manufacturer supplying wholesalers or retailers should perhaps promote sales to these intermediaries rather than the end consumer.

Promotional work as covered in this Chapter can be enormously successful in generating business. Situations when such promotions should be considered include:

1. The launch of a new product or service, especially if it is innovative and you need to make a special effort to educate prospective customers.
2. To counter a competitor's activities.
3. To maintain sales levels.
4. To increase your market share.

The general public has been subjected to such a flood of promotional gimmicks in recent years that it has become very blasé. Really effective consumer promotion today is therefore more difficult to achieve. Trade buyers are not quite so saturated but are more cynical so a trade-orientated promotion must be genuine to succeed.

Here are some promotional techniques:

Mailshots Possibly one of the most common promotional techniques is the simple mailshot. These are used for selling to both consumer and trade customers. A mailshot can consist of a personalised letter, a letter introducing an enclosed brochure or sample or simply a 'circular' (ie a leaflet which is not addressed to anyone in particular).

Usually the most effective is the carefully thought out personalised letter, where not only is the address and salutation personalised but the content is specific to the recipient.

With circulars an effective form is one that includes several different items, rather than one big brochure (as the reader is more likely to look through the separate items). If doing repeat mailshots, do vary the envelopes & contents or recipients will begin to recognise them and may discard without reading.

Samples This can be effective in two particular circumstances: a) where the recipient of the free sample is a decision-maker with the potential to place repeat orders or b) where the recipient is an "opinion-leader", ie an influential person who may not place an order, but can influence others who will.

The sample requires a covering letter and should be followed-up.

Open Days If you have an office or workshop which is something you can be proud of then consider showing it off with an Open Day. Make certain there is plenty to see, the event is well publicised beforehand, refreshments are laid on, staff are briefed as to how they should handle visitors and security is organised (to prevent pilfering). A practical example of preparing and running an Open Day is given opposite.

Free Gifts Whereas a sample is an example of your product which you want to promote, the Free Gift is a different concept. One type is a useful item (usually business-orientated for trade buyers) with the provider's company name emblazoned on it and its function is to keep the company's name or brand name at the forefront of the potential buyer's mind. The choice of such gifts is enormous with prices to suit. There are companies whose sole business is the production of these promotional gift items. To find their names and more information about promotional gifts, there are a number of trade magazines — refer to BRAD (see page 59).

Free Gifts for trade buyers are usually distributed at some special event, eg at a Trade Show; Open Day at the company's premises or showrooms; Launch Ceremony for some new product; Opening Ceremony at new premises, or at Christmas time. Such gifts can be effective but 5 golden rules should be borne in mind:
1. They should be such that they will be used frequently by potential buyers, and not be put straight in the bin.
2. They should have your company name (and, space permitting, a selling message and contact information, just like any other advertisement).

PAUL HUXFORD'S MINI DAY

One of Rover's dealerships, Paul Huxford at Fareham, provides a textbook example of how they ran a successful Open Day.

First the objective was defined. The company wanted a promotion which would bring in a large number of new customers. The option they plumped for was a Sunday Open Day — with the theme of "Mini Day".

Basing the promotion on a Mini gave immediate advantages in public appeal — and in addition a new model had just been launched. Detailed planning started 6 weeks before the event. Arrangements were scaled on the assumption of at least 1,000 visitors during the day, with enough displays, competitions and demonstrations to keep the prospects interested for a minimum of an hour. Children's amusements were also essential as this would be a Sunday family event.

On show would be various historic Minis, racing Minis, the latest new models and the Huxford Mini X, making its debut. This last, billed as the ultimate special edition Mini, was a fire-breathing 1400cc Mini with luxury trim and equipment. Creating their own display were mini-owners, who were invited to take part in competitions such as one for the cleanest and one for the "tattiest Mini still on the road" — but *everyone* who arrived in a Mini received a souvenir prize. The local Motor Club was invited to put on an hourly precision driving test display, after which guests could compete for a prize. Two initially identical Minis were carefully prepared for a "Spot the Difference Competition".

To promote their Workshop Service, there was a Mini plug-changing competition against the clock and an imaginative combined Bodyshop tour with a colour-matching competition. Huxford also took the opportunity to launch a new valet service, with a special offer of a steam clean with car wash for visitors. Another attraction was the offer of a 10-point safety check for customers who wanted to look underneath their cars and perhaps bring them back to have work done later.

To promote car sales, in addition to the special Minis and the normal product range display, the showroom was buzzing with an appropriate "Swinging Sixties" fashion show, put on by local students. Partly as an insurance against bad weather, there was also a large Scalextric track, backed up by computer driving games, set up in the showroom.

Perhaps the hardest part of such a promotion was deciding how to publicise it. Too much advertising is wasteful, but too little could mean a poor turn out and a wasted promotion. Tickets were despatched to every customer on their mailing list. Local advertising was carried out for two weeks before the event, building it up by including it in routine used car ads and in the "What's On" classified ads. A radio ad used the dramatic scenario of a Mini driving away by itself, followed by another 30 second spot in the next break giving details of the promotion. To help boost attendance, Huxford invited a celebrity, Alan Ball, Portsmouth Football Club Manager and full details of the Open Day were sent by Press Release to the local media for editorial coverage, stressing Alan Ball's involvement.

On the day itself, Minis started to arrive an hour before the official start time and the day's total topped 200. Nearly 2,000 people came during the day (twice that planned for) and over 700 free ice creams were dispensed. Over 100 test drives were carried out and by Monday, there were 20 orders. When the last guest had departed, the promotion didn't stop there of course — a Press Release was issued on Monday to describe the event!

Article by kind permission of Paul Huxford and Newslink Magazine

Promoting Sales

3. The gifts should, wherever possible, have a connection with your company's product or service, however slight.

4. The gifts should be durable with a lifetime of at least several months.

5. Note there are tax implications. Business gifts other than free samples of your own product are not normally allowable as a deduction for tax purposes. However gifts that include a prominent advertisement and worth less than a set value (currently £10) may be eligible (though food and drink are excluded). Ask you accountant for more details.

Another type of business Free Gift which appears mainly at Christmas time is the bottle of whisky, perfume, chocolates or whatever. It is different from the previous category in that it rarely carries the gift provider's company name, is usually a luxury consumable and is not directly business-related. They are sometimes used as a "thank you" gesture for business placed in the past year, but their use in generating additional future sales is questionable.

A different type of Free Gift which is used increasingly in consumer promotions is one where the customer is given a nice, but usually quite cheap, gift as a "come-on" or "reward". The come-on might be a voucher which entitles the recipient to a gift if he or she visits your premises or perhaps visits and purchases goods worth over a specified amount.

Free Lunches Someone once said there is no such thing as a "free lunch!" They could be right. The concept of a business meeting over a meal seems an attractive one at first sight but all too many seem to go on too long, too much time is spent on non-productive chat, nobody bothers to take any notes, few real decisions are made and it is expensive! The net result being that the only profits that are increased are those of the restaurateur. Arranging to see an important client over a meal can be a useful activity but some of the above points should be borne in mind.

Discounting This can be a sensitive issue. Discounts on published prices fall into several categories — there are those discounts which are openly quoted for special category buyers, eg pensioners, students etc. Then there are commercially confidential discounts which are offered to, or demanded by, large purchasing organisations. Finally there is incentive discounting which is offered by a salesperson to close a sale. If you have calculated the prices correctly then any discount means reduced profit which is a bad thing so discounts should be given judiciously and for a specific purpose. If you have to discount heavily on a continual basis it is a clear indicator that something is wrong somewhere, eg your normal prices are too high for the market, or intense competition or lack of demand is forcing prices down.

Sales This is a specialised form of discounting and was traditionally to clear old stock before new stock arrived. In the retail sector "Sales" have become a promotional tool and take place frequently for all sorts of excuses, mainly to increase volume sales or market share, or to improve poor sales figures. Their usefulness in the consumer market in generating sales activity has reduced due to excessive use and some abuse. For example one major national retailer recently promoted a Sale with adverts claiming *everything* was in the sale but in fact most items were discounted by less than one per cent!.

In contrast, when selling to trade buyers, sales can still be very effective particularly if they are genuine, eg end-of-line or old model equipment, display-soiled or whatever.

Two-for-Price-of-One Another form of discount is the "two for the price of one" or "buy ten, get one free" or "20% extra free in this packet" type of promotion. Used to excess by supermarket chains on food and some toiletry lines it has lost some of its edge. A more sophisticated version is the "buy so many and win a (desirable) prize" type of promotion.

Presentations These can be very profitable indeed if you are speaking to the *right* people (ie potential buyers) and you can speak convincingly. Like the Fashion Show (below) you have a captive audience. This idea can be used for many different businesses covering manufacturing, service industries, trade buyers or consumers. All you need to do is think very carefully who your likely buyers might be then invite them to an occasion where you can have their undivided attention and give them your sales "pitch".

To get the buyers to come you must make the occasion sound interesting and appealing — you should choose an attractive location, perhaps a major hotel, and you may think about offering food and drink as an incentive for people to come. If you are selling to trade buyers then if you can set up the talk through a trade association or Chamber of Commerce so much the better — you may even be able to tag onto some other event.

HINTS FOR DOING A PROFESSIONAL PRESENTATION

BEFOREHAND

Venue Find and book a suitable room which is large enough, has comfortable seats and is suitable for any sound/video equipment you may require. Check also the ability to control the lighting and curtains on windows if showing slides, videos etc. Does it need a microphone? An empty room may carry a voice easily to the back but full of people the sound is absorbed and the audience creates background noise too.

Speakers Who is to speak? Have they done public speaking before? They may be very knowledgeable but ill-suited to speaking. Does it need more than one speaker (this gives variety and is usually better). Specify dress.

Talk Whoever is speaking needs to know precisely what they are supposed to be speaking about and how long they have to speak. The talk should be written out, rehearsed on colleagues and any visuals (slides or video) should be run through. The talks should be 5-15 minutes each, 30 minutes only exceptionally.

Visual Aids You can help to keep the audience's attention by using lots of visual aids, eg 35mm slides, overhead projector (OHP), video and/or flip-chart. Better still use a combination of these. Slides and OHPs should not just echo what someone is saying or be endless lists of words...they should be pictures or possibly graphs. If using 35mm slides, a spare bulb for the projector is essential. Videos have a tendency to be too long.

Invites Ensure the invitations (with RSVP) are sent out in plenty of time. Remember to mention refreshments.

Refresh-ments What refreshments are planned? Who will provide them? Who will serve them and clear-up later? Do you want them before, after or in the middle of the presentation? What's your budget?

Staffing Who will welcome the guests, take their coats and handle any visual aid equipment? Name tags for staff is a good idea. Remember name boards for the speakers too.

THE PRESENTATION ITSELF

Arrival It is sensible to arrive in plenty of time to sort out inevitable last minute hitches. Have a checklist to tick off that everything is as planned.

The Talk If nervous, it is better to read from a script than to ad lib and make a mess of it. If reading, pause now and then to look up and get some eye contact. Speak as if you were addressing someone at the rear of the room. Many people tend to speak too quickly, so slow down and try not to move your hands too much as that can be distracting.

Formality Depending on the audience and the occasion, the presentation can either be very formal or more relaxed. One way to relax the event is for the speaker to remove his or her jacket at the start of the talk and to sit or stand immediately in front of the audience rather than be behind a lectern or desk.

Timing Try to start on time, even if people are still slipping in or have not yet arrived. Most people talk for too long — arrange some system, eg a prod from a colleague when the speaker should be coming to a close.

Questions Allow time for questions. This can be immediately after each speaker or all at the end or a bit of both.

Display At the end of the Presentation, useful additional mileage from the event can be gained from handing out relevant company brochures to the people attending and having at the side or back of the room a display of products/photos or whatever, perhaps with other staff on hand to answer any questions.

Promoting Sales

If you are going to all this effort then it obviously makes sense to ensure your presentation is top notch — see the previous page.

Coupons/Tokens These take a variety of forms from the tokens you might get when buying petrol which when saved can be exchanged for a gift, to coupons which allow x% off the next purchase, and so on. These are calculated to generate repeat business so work best with national chains and heavy supporting advertising budgets. They are therefore likely to be of less relevance to the small business.

Competitions/Raffles There are two main problems here. First, coming up with a competition or raffle that will catch the buyer's attention. Again the pressures on High Street retailing have seen this promotional device used heavily and people's expectations of prizes are now beyond what most small businesses can justify. Second, there are a considerable number of regulations relating to the running of these promotions. Get legal advice first.

In-store Demos If you are offering a consumer service or product, then the opportunity of doing an in-store demonstration in a large store should not be missed. There has to be something in it for the store too, for instance they may be selling your product in one Department. If the product you are demonstrating is a bit dull to the average person, then you can make the demo more attractive by hiring a celebrity to help. You should then make the most of this by publicising the event with advertising and a Press Release. If the product is new then this can give you valuable market research feedback.

Free Trial Another way of demonstrating a product is where the potential customer is offered a free trial. This can cover quite a range of products such as cars, business machines, computers, Hi-Fi sound systems etc.

Newsletter This is a sophisticated promotional tool. It is best used when you have a wide range of products or services to talk about and your customers cover a wide range of trade sectors so that communicating through an existing trade publication is difficult. As with a Press Release it should not read like one long advertisement. That would lose it any credibility. It should instead talk about other people and other firms (who could be your customers), with the occasional reference to your own products or services.

Fashion Show This can be done in-store or at any other suitable venue and is appropriate for all apparel and accessories. It is only effective if it attracts a big enough audience and they are potential buyers. Putting on such a show is much more difficult than it looks, requiring experienced models, proper lighting and sound, choreography, rehearsals, ticket sales (or distribution, if free) and good promotion — just for starters! Often related but non-competitor businesses can join together to put on a bigger, and therefore more attractive, show. The audience needs *entertaining* not just shown an endless parade of garments (hence the need for professional choreography and props). The objective is to *sell* so a commentator should be used to describe the garments and accessories as they are modelled. A sales leaflet can be placed on each seat before the guests arrive. A video taken of the event (or of a rehearsal) can be used to promote sales in your own showroom later.

Videos Where you are trying to convey a complex visual message or perhaps show something working or moving which is too large to bring with you, then showing a video of it can be a very persuasive sales promotional tool. The two things to avoid are showing a very amateur video or one that runs too long (several minutes is ideal and anything over 10 or 15 minutes is probably too long for most situations). For a professional video team to make a video it used to cost about £1000 per minute of final film. These prices have dropped but it is still expensive to do properly and you also have to consider how the video is going to be shown.

Link-ups The idea of joining other businesses as described in the Fashion Show above is one useful form of link-up. It may also take the form of distributing each others leaflets or referring customers to each other if the two businesses are complementary (eg one may be a retailer selling wedding dresses, another operating limousines for hire). Another example is where a small firm rides on the back of a larger (non-competitor) corporation. The relationship has to be of benefit to both parties and can take a number of forms, such as the larger firm allowing the smaller firm to take a subsidised advert in its in-house magazine.

Fraud A final point is whatever incentive scheme you run, you must check that it cannot be defrauded by your customers or staff ∎

PLANNING
& SPECIAL SITUATIONS

Chapters

MARKETING & SALES PLAN

A significant factor that distinguishes successful businesses from those that are less so is the degree of planning that is carried out. It must be said that many small businesses are guilty of doing very little planning, usually because the proprietors either feel they "don't have the time" or they may think "it's not worth it — we know what we are doing".

A business that does no planning or insufficient planning is often characterised by crises, "unexpected" problems, too much management time spent sorting out the day-to-day problems and generally a great deal of trauma.

When a business starts, there is a tendency to chase every possible avenue for sales without a very clear sales plan in mind other than a vague notion that one must work to achieve a large turnover and achieve it as quickly as possible.

In the early stages of a new business there is so much to do it is not surprising that there is little to no time for long term planning. Anyway, it is difficult to produce a meaningful plan as things are still too new — there is not enough track record on which to base future predictions with any degree of accuracy. But after you have been trading for a year or so, you will find that time spent on planning can be worthwhile financially (ie it can indicate how you can make more money!). Perhaps even more importantly it can give you great peace of mind to know *where* you are, *where* you are going, *how* you might get there and that things seem generally under control.

The plan you produce should not simply be done, filed and forgotten. It should be thought of as akin to a route map and referred to regularly (at least every few months). This will allow you to see what progress you are making, if your various calculations, such as pricing, are still OK, if you had remembered all your good ideas and so on.

A Specialised Business Plan

You will probably be familiar with Business Plans and in fact you might have completed one before you started your own business. Looking back you may think that was a rather theoretical exercise because of the difficulty of predicting with any certainty how the business was going to operate in its first year. You might have used your Business Plan to raise some start-up finance but perhaps you never referred to it again as events took a different turn from that predicted in the Plan (a not unusual occurrence).

The Marketing & Sales Plan can be considered as a specialised form of Business Plan. As this new Plan is based on actual trading results for a year or more, it should be much more realistic and useful. The more effort you put into producing the Plan, the more you are likely to get out of it.

You will note it is called a Marketing & Sales Plan rather than a Sales & Marketing Plan. This is a little subtlety to stress that you first need to decide on the overall marketing strategy before working out the minutiae of the sales tactics.

Unlike the Business Plan which would have been seen by a number of people such as your Bank Manager, accountant and business advisers, the Marketing & Sales Plan can be an entirely private document for your eyes only.

Annual & Mini Plans

A Plan ought to be done every year. This could either be in January

"Be interesting to see how she flies .... the Brits designed the wings in feet, while the Europeans made the rest in metres ...."

Planning

MARKETING & SALES PLAN

I THE PAST YEAR

The first part of the Plan should be a brief account of the past year, highlighting the main events, including both successes and failures. It is fascinating to look back on these events and much can be learned from them for the future.

II OBJECTIVES

Any Plan must have an objective or, more likely, several objectives. This should be a short statement, probably no longer than a paragraph or two. It could be an objective in terms of turnover, or better still, net profit for the next year. It might also include several objectives such as "open a new shop in town X" or "develop Product Y for launch in May" or "reduce overheads by 10%" or whatever. All assumptions should be stated! It is always better to be modest in your goals since their achievement acts as an encouragement whereas if you fail to achieve a more ambitious goal it makes one a little despondent.

III PRODUCT/SERVICE PLAN

This part of the Plan runs through what the business is doing today and describes its products or services. Although at first it may seem superfluous to write down your business's activities, the exercise does put the matter into sharp perspective and throws up the odd gem.

IV MARKET RESEARCH DATA

This is really just a few lines or paragraphs on the salient points of the most recent market information. You should also make a comment about the market predictions for the next year, your customers and the competition.

V PRICING

This should be a summary enclosing your latest pricing calculations with perhaps a note on your competitor's prices too.

VI SALES PLAN

This should be a more lengthy statement on how the sales are to be achieved to meet the sales targets mentioned in Noll above. This should look at distribution, responsibilities, monitoring and sales strategies.

VII PROMOTIONS PLAN

This part should start with a calculation on how much the promotional budget should be for the forthcoming year to achieve the sales targets. It should be a comprehensive plan to include any advertising, PR and other promotions such as Exhibitions, together with a note on their budgeted costs, timescales and monitoring.

VIII CASHFLOW FORECAST

Finally, and perhaps most importantly, the Plan should have a Cashflow Forecast for the year ahead. Once prepared, this should be updated monthly during the year. This is a key part of the Plan. A small PC computer with a spreadsheet program allows one to do cashflows quickly and easily.

covering January to December or it might match your financial year, whichever you prefer. An advantage of it matching your financial year is that it is easier to incorporate some of the financial details from your annual accounts. A 12-month period is probably the right timescale as it will reflect any seasonal variations and yet not be looking too far into the future.

Whereas the Annual Plan lays down the overall strategy for the business for the next year, there are other occasions which might require Mini Plans. Such occasions might be a major opportunity that had not been foreseen when the Annual Plan was written, the sudden appearance of a hostile competitor or any other event which is significant enough to upset the original Plan. Such a Mini Plan can be quite a modest document — a page or two of thoughts and conclusions which are attached inside the Annual Plan.

Producing The Plan

The actual contents of the Plan will depend entirely on the particular business, its circumstances and how you want to do your planning. Some common elements are noted opposite with appropriate comments.

An important reason for doing the Plan is to ensure all the different parts of the business are integrated, ie if you get a good response to an ad but have no capability to follow it up properly then the expense and effort going into the advertising will be wasted. OK, we all know that in reality things will not necessarily work out as planned, but even so there will be a lot to gain from starting on the right footing!

As to the physical form of the Plan, it needs to be flexible so the pages of hand-written or typed notes and calculations could be inserted in a ring binder or file.

Although your plan may be private, it is probably appropriate to discuss with your key staff where you plan to take the business in the forthcoming year.

What Can A Plan Highlight?

The sort of plan you produce might highlight the following:

1. Which aspects of your business are more profitable and hence should be those which are promoted more strongly in future. Equally it should indicate what activities are a dead loss.

2. Where you might have tried something but it did not work out quite as expected, the plan can often clarify what you did wrong.

3. The *strengths* and *weaknesses* of your business (but do try to be honest with yourself).

4. The opportunities for your business and the potential threats from market changes and competitors.

Producing the Plan encourages you to take the time to do a review of your whole business at least once a year.

And a final thought on the subject of planning: *"Planning is a sign of a business maturing and becoming established"*■

Solving A Cashflow Problem

Unfortunately, this is a situation that confronts many businesses, particularly newish ones, and if not handled correctly it might well lead to the premature demise of the venture. The phrase "cashflow problems" can cover a whole variety of ailments but their net effect is to cause the business to run out of funds so bills cannot be met. Relatively new businesses with their high start-up costs and lowish sales are particularly vulnerable.

But cashflow problems can also afflict very successful businesses too.

Detection

First of all, you have to be aware that there is a problem as this may not be so obvious in its early stages, particularly if accounts books are not fully up to date as everyone has been 'too busy'. One of the best indicators is a Cashflow Forecast which is continually failing to meet its forecasts.

A Cashflow Forecast is just what it says, ie a forecast of cash flowing in and out of the business (on a monthly basis) usually for 12 months ahead (though in a crisis, one might need to consider the cashflow on a weekly basis). All forecast sales (and any other income, eg grants) are incorporated in the Cashflow together with predicted expenses (rent, rates, wages, stock etc).

How to produce a Cashflow Forecast and manage your business finances effectively using Cashflow Management techniques is covered in detail in a companion book, titled *The (Greatest) Little Business Book*.

If you did a "break-even" Cashflow Forecast where your predicted sales just match your outgoings and then found that the actual trading results were falling below these thresholds, you would know that the business is trading at a loss. In any business, sales go through peaks and troughs which may be seasonal in character but with a properly prepared Cashflow Forecast it will still be possible to spot an adverse trading situation.

The great advantage of Cashflow Management is that it should provide very early warning of any cashflow problems thereby allowing maximum time and room to manoeuvre. If nothing is done the situation will deteriorate and one or a number of classic warning signals may become evident. These are: a) a rising overdraft level (without any specific reason); b) increasing difficulties in paying trade creditors and c) falling behind in the monthly PAYE/NIC tax payments.

These are all very serious signs of impending disaster and demand immediate action. Once a cashflow problem is detected it is vital to have a complete and up-to-date financial picture. A Cashflow Forecast should immediately be prepared together with lists of outstanding creditors and debtors and a further note or list relating to orders or sales likely to materialise in the next few weeks or months. As the business is in trouble we are looking at short time spans.

Analysis

Cashflow Problems can occur due to either one, or worse, a combination of five main factors:
1. Sales Levels — too low.
2. Overheads — too high.
3. Profit Margins — too small.
4. Debtors — too slow (or not paying!).
5. Trading Level — too great.
It is important to identify clearly which factor or factors are relevant in your own case — it may be fairly self-evident! Let us look at each one in turn.

LOW SALES

Having a low turnover is an endemic problem with new (ie under 2-3 years old) small businesses and there are several reasons for this. Many businesses are set up with much optimism, insufficient knowledge of the market and too little capital. Another factor, closely related to this, is that it takes time, often a great deal of time, to become established and this period is normally much longer than most initial Business Plans allow. The problem is, of course, not solely the preserve of new businesses for an established business facing changes in the market may experience falling sales if it does not respond.

If, as a newish business, you are experiencing low sales figures the key question to face is then "Is this a sound business proposition which just needs more time or capital to become established?" The answer might be no! For an established business it may be that sales are dropping or sales have remained fixed while overheads have risen. The product or service being offered may no longer be suitable for the market.

The important thing is you must do something! Once a low sales level situation is diagnosed you must move fast as the business will be growing weaker and there will be less time to make changes and fewer options available. So what are the options?

Option 1: Increase Sales

There is hardly a business in existence which at one time or another has not presented its proprietors or Directors with the dilemma of how to increase sales to rectify an adverse cashflow

Solving A Cashflow Problem

problem. People tend to react to this in two ways, either completely ignoring the problem as they simply cannot face the awfulness of it (and they are unsure what to do) or they over react and institute panic measures which are ill-considered and potentially damaging. In most peoples' minds questions fly around – should they advertise more? Should they cut their prices? Should they sack their staff? Should they ....??

The only sensible course of action is first to analyse the situation you are in, second to consider the options, third to draw up a plan and fourth to try to carry it out. OK, you say, that sounds easy on paper – but it is not suggested that this is going to be easy, just that this is a way to tackle the problem.

The first decision to make is how to give yourself some time. When a business is not going smoothly the demands on you can increase, making the finding of "thinking" time seem difficult if not impossible. But if the business is facing a crisis you simply *must* make time – one practical suggestion is to set aside one hour before you start work each day to concentrate your full energy on the problem (most people are more alert in the morning and the day's dramas have not yet intruded).

Analysis And Actions Analysis is the most critical activity and attempts to answer why the current sales levels are low. Low turnover means too few customers and/or each customer is spending too little. In all this work, write down a summary of your thoughts and conclusions. This is really most important for if left "in the head" it can become very confused and contradictory.

Look again carefully at each step in the selling process:

1. Seeking Customers Ask yourself how you expect people to hear about your business and then try asking some how they actually heard about you. How many people do you need to hear about you to sensibly provide enough enquiries so that actual sales will be sufficient? Few small businesses promote themselves adequately due to lack of time, money (and probably expertise). But simply deciding to "spend more on advertising" is not necessarily the right answer and in any event your business may not be able to afford much advertising in its present state. If you need to find more customers, re-read the previous section of this book, on 'Advertising, Promotion & Sales'.

2. Stimulating Their Interest It may be that sufficient customers are aware of you but their interest has not been caught. Your company or its products may not look up-to-date enough, or they may look too up-market or too down-market, for most of your potential customers. Try speaking to people who are not making a purchase, some will be honest enough to give you an answer and this may be illuminating. Look again at the competition – what are they doing successfully which you are not?

3. Satisfying Their Needs If your product or service is different from your competitors, pencil quickly a little table comparing your product or service with your competitors. Maybe you include a feature which is putting off potential buyers or missing a feature which your competitors are offering. Though, of course, your competitors may not be right either! Also, your business may be projecting one image but the bulk of its stock may be more suitable for a different image. Price is of crucial importance in a number of trade sectors, so ensure your price is correct. Again, talking to people will shed some light on this aspect.

4. Selling Sometimes the product or service is right, the customer is ready to make the purchase but the actual sales technique being used is simply inadequate or even off-putting. Not everyone is a good, natural salesperson and selling does require its own persuasive skills, knowledge and enthusiasm even when the product or service is itself excellent.

If any one of these aspects is not quite right, that is where to concentrate your initial efforts. See the relevant Chapters earlier in this book for more information.

Option 2: Change The Deal
In many cases the analysis will reveal several flaws – a need for greater promotion and possibly a need for some material change to the product or service on offer to make it more saleable. Due to your cashflow predicament there may be a temptation to do something really drastic in terms of changing the product or service on offer, but it is probably much safer to be evolutionary rather than revolutionary. So in essence try to stick to what you are doing but make a number of fine adjustments and check the response to each of those. These small changes can be implemented much quicker, at much lower cost and involve much lower risk.

Almost any action you take will require some additional cash and this is covered on page 110 under the heading RE-FINANCING.

If all the steps in the selling process

Solving A Cashflow Problem

are genuinely being done *reasonably* well (and there is little point in kidding yourself if this is not the case) then the truth may be there is insufficient demand for your product or service as it currently stands. In that case one might consider Option 3.

Option 3: Diversify

It may be that your initial market research was not quite spot-on and the market is really looking for a completely different product or service, or a major adaptation of what you are currently offering. This is not an unusual situation. However, calm consideration needs to be given to this option as change or diversification on this scale must be thought of as akin to an entirely new project, almost like setting up a new venture from scratch. Thus it will take time and money to establish and may mean venturing into uncharted waters.

Diversification should not be seen as a panacea to your current problems, however it can be very successful if carried out with due market research and especially if allied to what the business is currently doing, thereby building on the contacts and business knowledge which have already been acquired.

Brain-Storming To come up with a diversified product or service, try a "brain-storming" session. To do this, get away from the work environment and take your fellow partners, Directors, key staff or other confidant(e)s. You could probably use a sitting room in one of your homes, provided it is large enough and peaceful, or if that is not possible, hire a small function room in a local Hotel. Ensure that lots of coffee and sandwiches are on hand and that

there are absolutely no interruptions. The session should start in the morning when everyone is fresh and it may last until mid or even late afternoon. The "rules" of the session are that people come up with as many ideas as they can but are never criticised or ridiculed by the others, however "wild" an idea may seem at first. This tends to encourage the more unusual ideas and some lateral thinking. If there are more than three or four people in the group it might also be useful to have a large piece of paper or flip-chart which everyone can see and on which all the ideas are written. After a few hours the group can switch from generating fresh ideas to looking in more detail at those already thrown up and by the end of the session there should be a number of ideas to be followed up as "possibles". All these ideas should be recorded, in summarised form, for any future sessions.

HIGH OVERHEADS

It may be that the business concept is basically sound but more time is needed to allow the business to reach its potential trading levels or overheads have unexpectedly risen (perhaps due to a recent rent review on the premises). There are obviously two ways out of this predicament — the first is to attempt to increase sales to cover the higher overheads. Such a strategy might be correct if the higher overheads were in some way "justifiable".

The second way out of the predicament is to reduce your overheads. If the other factors to be considered (ie Sales Levels, Profit Margins and Debtors) are reasonably in line with your Cashflow Forecast, then you can concentrate on reducing overheads to a level that the business can sustain. In

most small businesses the two largest overheads are staff wages and/or the rent and rates of the premises. Some businesses may also carry large finance charges particularly if they needed to purchase a lot of stock or equipment.

Look at your staffing needs carefully. Several options may be possible. First, can you do with fewer staff who would each work longer hours? Or can the business survive with the existing staff working fewer hours? Many businesses carry very junior staff whose productivity is often low and who may require a great deal of supervision. It may be better to have fewer, higher quality staff. In some cases, if the situation facing the business is spelled out, staff may accept a lower fixed wage with a bonus based on their sales or other quantifiable output, especially if redundancy is the stark alternative.

A completely different approach may be to use outside freelance workers, or "temps", or to contract out parts of your work. Many small businesses feel they must have a secretary because the boss cannot type and they need someone to "look after the office and answer the phone". This may be a luxury the business cannot afford and a telephone answering machine plus a typing service will fill the gap almost as well and at a fraction of the cost. However, with the ready availability of cheap yet powerful small business computers, most bosses should seriously consider learning to type their own letters anyway as well as to use the computers for other functions such as Cashflow Forecasts.

If planning to make staff redundant, remember that if they have been employed in the business continuously for 2 years or more, then they are entitled to redundancy payments. It is

Solving A Cashflow Problem

therefore essential to get professional advice before you take any action.

In terms of premises, if trading from factory premises, consider moving to smaller or less "prime" premises if your lease permits. This may also apply to office space. In both cases, as an alternative your landlord may allow you to sub-let part temporarily to give you some income (ie effectively to reduce your rental burden) but this would require the landlord's express permission as most leases forbid such sub-letting. Shops present more of a problem as the site is so important and moving to smaller or less well placed premises may well be an unwise move.

Finance charges are covered below in the section Re-Financing. See also the box "Keeping Overheads Down" in the Chapter **Pricing**.

Finance charges can be significant where a lot of money is tied up in stock and even if sales are hitting their targets, if the stock levels are relatively excessive (ie the stock is slow moving) then this can cause cashflow problems.

Finally, a totally avoidable yet all too frequent cause of cashflow problems is caused by the proprietor(s) simply drawing out too much cash for themselves from their business. This is sometimes because no thought has been given to make provision to pay for VAT, tax etc.

SQUEEZED PROFIT MARGINS

Margins may be lower than anticipated for a variety of reasons – the need to discount heavily (possibly due to competition); rises in raw material or stock costs which cannot be passed on immediately to customers; exchange rate fluctuations (when you are importing or exporting). Another problem is

---

DEBT RECOVERY STRATEGY

At time of supply	Provide Invoice (specifying payment due date)
At end of month	Send Statement
About 2 weeks after payment due	Phone and speak to Accounts Dept (and note name of person who looks after your account)
+ 1-2 weeks	Phone again and speak to same person
+ 1-2 weeks	Send polite letter "Recorded Delivery"
+ 1 week	Phone and try to speak to boss
+ ?	If possible, visit in person, or send more direct letter
+ ?	Consider legal proceedings if amount of debt makes this step worthwhile

---

that even though you may be making sales at your normal full price, these prices may themselves be too low, allowing inadequate margin to sustain the business. Refer to the Chapter **Pricing** again.

Many businesses offer a variety of products and services which have different profit margins. This gives them the opportunity to switch slowly from low margin work to that which has the higher margins. This simple and gentle change in marketing strategy may mean a temporary decrease in turnover but an increase in overall profitability of the business, especially if overheads are reduced to match the initially lower level of trading.

Another point to note is that even if your margins are typical for your trade, you should always work at increasing them by a few percentage points here and there, wherever possible, as cumulatively this can add up to a useful increase in profit.

BAD PAYERS

Slow payment by customers (or worse, non-payment) is a business malady we regrettably seem to have to learn to live

with and almost every business needs to spend time pursuing bad payers. Small businesses are particularly vulnerable as they are often under-capitalised and in their eagerness to get a sale or win a contract may turn a blind eye to the credit worthiness of the buyer. The situation is aggravated by some large well-funded corporations using their supplier companies as a flexible (and free) source of credit finance!

If you already have a problem with bad payers a suggested Debt Recovery strategy as outlined in the box above might be considered but the important point is to minimise future exposure to such risks. Proper credit checks should be carried out on all customers requiring credit over a threshold you feel relevant, for instance it may not be worth the effort in a trade-to-trade context proving credit worthiness if your maximum exposure per customer is under, say £50. Credit checks should include the customer's bank and at least two other suppliers. Whereas the bank can give an indication of the *ability* of the company to pay, the other suppliers will give a clue as to their

Solving A Cashflow Problem

willingness to pay! The almost irresistible temptation to take a big order from an unproven and possible credit risk customer should always be avoided.

Debt recovery from overseas customers present different and sometimes difficult problems. Refer to the section on Exporting earlier in this book.

Risk Reduction

Other ways to reduce your exposure include spreading the risk, ie more small customers rather than several big ones (though the administration time rises dramatically); payment by pro-forma invoice (ie payment in advance); taking a deposit; splitting large orders into several smaller deliveries each of which has to be paid before the next part of the order is despatched; and the use of Factoring (see opposite).

Credit Checking Agencies

In addition to doing your own credit checks, you might also use a reputable credit checking agency. One well known supplier of business information reports for credit checking and risk management purposes, founded about 150 years ago, is Dun & Bradstreet.

When a firm is considering supplying a company on credit then it can ask Dun & Bradstreet for a report on that company to see how credit-worthy it is. A range of business information reports are immediately available via D&B's online telephone, faxed or mailed services. You can choose precisely the level of report you require for a particular decision from overview to in-depth analytical information. Each of D&B's key information reports include the unique D&B Rating and "maximum credit recommendation" to help you to assess the level of risk associated with a company and to set credit limits.

The D&B Comprehensive Report is presented in an easy-to-read format yet packed with essential data. It includes the D&B Rating, a highly predictive indicator of business failure and an objective assessment of the financial strength and risk level associated with the business and the "maximum credit recommendation". In addition it confirms key officers and identifies their other Directorships, enables you to appraise payment trends, review any County Court Judgements and provides business indicators with summarised accounts, financial comparisons and performance ratios. Sections giving press cuttings and management comments add essential background information.

This information is drawn from a database with details on nearly 3 million UK businesses, both large and small (plus about 14 million European companies). The database is updated daily by personal interviews, questionnaires, a computer link from Companies House, County Courts and through subscribers themselves providing confidential information on how well they are being paid.

Although D&B information is available on a one-off basis for around £50 for a single report, some customers opt to have a year's contract and in doing so benefit from substantial discounts. Trial subscriptions are also available.

Dun & Bradstreet have regional offices (including Scotland) and their UK Head Office is at Holmers Farm Way, High Wycombe, Bucks HP12 4UL. For more information, tel: 061-832 6611.

OVER-TRADING

Another situation when cashflow problems can appear is when a company is expanding more rapidly than its available working capital allows. This situation therefore affects businesses that

would be regarded as "successful".

The business obviously has to either slow down or have more capital injected into it. (Note: Some of the comments on Re-Financing below do not strictly apply to a company that is over-trading).

RE-FINANCING

Sometimes businesses faced with cashflow problems seek to "remedy" them by looking for more cash to finance their increasing debt. The danger is, of course, self-evident in that the problem will not go away unless the root causes are tackled. However, even tackling these will often require some re-financing or restructuring of the present finances. This situation faces many businesses and it is not an easy task – there are probably few assets; the business may already be up to its maximum overdraft limit and its creditors will be knocking on the door for their money. The first step is to decide on a preferred course of action and its cost. A contingency factor should be allowed for, since if insufficient funds are raised it is most unlikely that you could re-finance again while the business is still in trouble. You usually only get one chance!

As the business is still trading, there are some things in its favour – its main creditors will normally be anxious to see the business continuing to trade and get over its problems. They have a vested interest in the venture which is more than just the immediate money it owes them. The Bank Manager does not want a failed business on his career record. Trade suppliers want to retain the "account" for the future, and Landlords do not want the expense of finding a new tenant. None of these people want the problems of the inevitable paperwork they will be faced with if your

Solving A Cashflow Problem

business fails especially if it ceases trading still owing them money. However, if they believe there is little hope in saving the situation they will not wish to pour good money after bad and would rather cut their losses. Many people put off telling their creditors that they are running into problems. This is quite natural but unfortunately, being kept in the dark, the creditors can panic. So you may need to keep them informed (but heed the two precautions below).

A Plan   A letter can outline your plan. It should clearly and confidently explain how you intend to correct the situation with their support. The plan should set modest goals which can be achieved for any failure to meet goals will be seen as a failure of the whole plan with dire consequences. The letter should be brief, though a Bank Manager (who is privy to your accounts anyway) will probably require more details. Any promises of repayments to creditors should be on modest timescales as they will lose confidence if any repayment is missed or late.

Two precautions must be stressed: a) you should not divulge any more of your business details than are absolutely essential and b) you must assume whoever you speak to will take whatever action is in *their* best interest not yours. If this presents a potential risk to you then only proceed with caution and first take impartial and professional advice.

Banks   Another catch is that a Bank will frequently refuse further cash (in the form of a loan or larger overdraft) unless some new capital, possibly equal to the bank's increased risk, is introduced into the business. For instance, if £6,000 is needed then the bank is unlikely to agree to more than

about £3,000 with the balance being new capital injected by some other party. This cash may come from one or a number of sources – the sale of some personal effects, re-mortgaging one's home, finding a new partner or shareholder, loans (on which interest should be paid) from friends or relatives etc. Sometimes where your product or service is unique and vital to the smooth operation of a large company who is a major customer of yours, that company may be prepared to make a loan (with interest) to keep you going, or to purchase a share-holding in your business. It can be a good method if the circumstances are right.

The provision of High Street finance to business is very competitive and many businesses facing a difficult time have moved their account (and their overdraft!) to a more amenable Bank Manager and this has helped with the recovery of the business.

Other Sources   For small businesses in trouble and requiring relatively small sums of money there are a variety of "lenders of last resort". These are often local government bodies and they may provide some cash (generally under £5,000) as part of a rescue package, provided there is good hope the business can be saved, and a sensible plan has been produced.

Finally, a business that is trading and has a fair chance of recovery should be able to raise the additional funds necessary to implement that recovery but only if a sensible Plan is produced.

Factoring
Another way of financing the business to ease cashflow problems is to make use of factoring, or "sales-linked funding" as it is sometimes called.

In this method, when you send an Invoice to your customer, you send a copy of the Invoice to the factor. Normally the factor then pays you 80% of the Invoice total almost immediately. The factor then takes the responsibility for chasing the debt, issuing statements and reminders. Your Invoice is annotated that the amount should be paid to the factor not yourself. When the Invoice is paid, you receive the balance from the factor (less their charges).

Factoring costs are broadly comparable with the cost of a bank overdraft, but has the advantage that the factor has the problem of chasing the debt.

SURVIVING A RECESSION

Recessions, as they affect small businesses, are more to do with a lack of consumer and business confidence than other factors. Even if there is 10% or 20% unemployment, there are still 80-90% *in* employment and the inherent wealth of a country does not just evaporate overnight. But what does happen is people become cautious and start to restrict their non-essential spending and this soon creates a recession.

The effects on a small business are soon obvious – turnover falls, stock levels rise, overheads become top-heavy and bad debts escalate. There are also side-effects, some of which may be a little unexpected. For instance, you may have increasing problems with the service you receive from your suppliers. This could be because they are holding less stock, have reduced their workforce and may be suffering from low staff morale. Less unexpected, banks and other financial institutions take a much harder line on lending, due to the bad debts they are suffering. And to cap it all, your competitors may start

Solving A Cashflow Problem

offering their products or services at ridiculously low prices just to keep the cash coming in.

The important point to grasp is that a small business has to swim with the tide. This is probably not the time for speculative ventures, expansion or increased expenditure. Whereas in times of no recession a business rightly gives emphasis to its SALES, when a recession occurs, a business should turn its attention more to managing its CASHFLOW. Provided you can control your cashflow to meet your bills, your business is in a good position to survive a recession.

Let us consider different ways to control your cash and conserve it (as it is always easier to save money than to earn it, particularly in a recession).

Advertising & Promotion In a recession people are simply not prepared to buy as they did before so increasing your advertising and promotion is less likely to bring a sufficient increase in sales to cover the extra cost. However, every effort should be made by you and your sales people to maximise sales.

Stock Levels These should be kept to the bare minimum. This is always difficult to estimate but, on balance, in a recession it is probably better to be close to running out of something than to have lots of unsold stock on your hands. When you are re-ordering, don't be tempted by discounts offered for volume purchase. Only buy what you know you can definitely sell even at reduced trading levels.

If you are a manufacturer, importer or shop-owner, then convert old stock into cash by attractive discounting. (You may also consider selling off any surplus or under-utilised assets).

Trading Level Your level of borrowing needs to be in tune with your trading, ie if you are growing on borrowings when the recession begins to bite you may be wiser to rein back a bit to reduce your borrowing requirements.

Borrowings It may be tempting to try to "solve" your problems by turning to hire purchase or other lenders when the bank will not increase your overdraft, but all you will be doing is increasing your overall debt which could be dangerous in these circumstances.

Debt Management First, tighten up your credit controls and if in any doubt ask for cash up-front. You also need to pursue all debtors (people who owe you money) vigorously, with special attention given to the biggest debts. Watch your major debtors like a hawk and move fast to get payment if you suspect that they may be in financial trouble. In addition, you probably need to pay your creditors only when payment is due, taking full advantage of any credit you have been offered. Request extended credit if necessary (this is more likely to be successful if you ask to pay half on the original due date and the balance at a specified time later, eg a further month. But don't abuse this privilege).

Overheads It is vital to reduce your overheads to a level which the existing (and forecast) sales of your business can support. The importance of this cannot be over-emphasised. (See the suggestions for reducing overheads on pages 33 and 108).

General Expenditure This is probably not the time to buy new capital goods (even if it is simply a new chair) or waste cash on sundry items. Try to make do with existing equipment and vehicles. Lock up your cheque book!

To know how successful your attempts to manage your cashflow have been (and just what you need to achieve) you need to practice Cashflow Management techniques, which are covered in detail in a companion book to this, ***The Greatest Little Business Book***.

In conclusion, a business in a recession should probably concentrate more on controlling its overheads rather than attempting to increase its sales. This is in fact the only thing that is completely under your control. And do remember to discuss the situation with your professional adviser, accountant or Local Enterprise Agency.

And take heart, all recessions eventually come to an end!

GETTING RID OF THE BUSINESS

If the prognosis is that the business cannot be made viable then you should plan to divest yourself of the venture in such a way as to minimise the losses. Even an unsuccessful business may be attractive to others or have assets which can be sold, so seek good professional advice at an early stage, your own accountant being the first to speak to.

If you have carefully nurtured a new business into life, owned one for many years or inherited one, it may be difficult to admit that things are not going well and that it is time to get rid of the business.

There are options to consider which will minimise the pain and allow you to retain some pride (and hopefully, some capital). If planned, the outcome can be as favourable as possible in the circumstances. It is worth noting that the American attitude to business "failure" is rather different to ours, seeing it as an opportunity to gain

Solving A Cashflow Problem

experience before starting the next venture.

Various options for getting rid of a business are:

1. To sell the business as a going concern Even a business that is trading at a loss may be of interest to others, so contact could be made with companies in your trade. These approaches can be made through a third party such as your solicitor or accountant. There are also Business Transfer Agents (see the Yellow Pages) who may be interested especially if the business falls into one of the following categories: Hotels, Pubs, Restaurants, Sub-Post Offices, NCTs (Newsagents', Confectioners' and Tobacconists'), General Stores and Rest/Nursing Homes. Other businesses, if they are retail may be of interest to them but generally they do not handle manufacturing type businesses. They operate on a commission basis when you appoint them to handle the sale of the business.

The value of a business is based on the following:
a) Stock: This is the value at cost price (ie it is not the retail price and it also excludes any VAT). You will notice that businesses for sale often say "plus SAV" which means the "Stock As Valued" at the time of the sale. Where the stock is large, it is usually valued independently to prevent disagreement.
b) Fixtures & Fittings: Again this is probably best valued independently and should take into account their depreciated value (see Note below).
c) Machinery & Equipment: These are valued like Fixtures & Fittings.
d) Goodwill: Whereas the above categories can be valued precisely (it can still lead to negotiations), goodwill is the really "grey" area of valuation.

Goodwill = Value of Business minus Business Assets. It is a measure of the momentum of profitability that the business has built up. It should therefore be based on the proven profit of the business, looking at the last few years. Since we are considering here a business that is trading at a loss, any Goodwill cannot really be based on a proven profit record. However, some goodwill may still be relevant based on other assets of the business which cannot be quantified elsewhere. For instance the business might own patents or a well-known trading name or have an exclusive agency for its territory or have an excellent customer (mailing) list or have staff with particular specialist skills. All these are of value to a purchaser and may therefore generate a goodwill payment over and above other payments for stock etc.

The total value of the business, ie what you may be able to sell it for, is the sum of the four factors above of which the last is the most negotiable. When selling a business there are usually tax implications which your accountant should advise you on, again to ensure you make the most from the sale.

Note: Depreciation is an accounting term which tries to put a life on an item. For instance, if the likely lifetime of a machine is 4 years, its value "depreciates" by 25% each year so if it cost £100 new, after a year its "accounts book" value would be £75, and after two years its value would be £75 less 25% and so on.

2. To split the business into smaller units By selling off any viable parts and simply closing or selling the remainder. This may include selling parts to your existing staff or to other companies. Within any business, even a very small "one-man" band operation, there may be parts which can be divested profitably.

3. To cease trading and sell off everything This is obviously a fairly drastic and final decision to make but may be the only course of action in the circumstances. Before doing anything get good professional advice. The timing of the cessation should be to your best advantage and the method of selling off one's assets needs as much planning as starting a new venture. Beware of the temptation to "switch off" and not face up to the painful decisions that have to be made.

There are legal implications which must be addressed when planning to cease trading so consult a solicitor at an early stage.

If you have an overdraft (which can be withdrawn at any time at the discretion of the Bank) this needs careful handling for if the Bank feels its overdraft might not be repaid, it may panic and withdraw the overdraft facility at short notice. This will simply exacerbate the whole situation.

Epitaph
Getting rid of a business need not be the end. Take heart, for many of today's high-profile and successful business people had a few failures in their early formative years. The invaluable "combat experience" you have gained will stand you in good stead should you wish to try another business venture.

One important lesson learned is that businesses are not always successful, a point that few if any new entrepreneurs ever consider or plan for ∎

Coping With Competitors

If a market is large enough to sustain more than one firm the appearance of a second firm can produce healthy competition, but if the market cannot support a new competitor then a most unhappy struggle will ensue. The situation may be worse still with many firms chasing too little business.

Almost every firm has competition but sometimes the real competition may not be easy to identify immediately. For instance, if the customers of a business are the general public, then potential competitors are any other business serving the same consumers as they are offering alternative ways for them to spend their disposable income. But let us consider first the direct competitor.

BENIGN COMPETITORS

There are various strategies for coping with competitors but the choice of strategy depends on whether you would assess any particular competitor as benign or hostile! A "benign" competitor could be described as one who keeps mainly to their own territory and/or shares the same customers, either keeping a stable market share or, if expanding, then at least not expanding at your expense. Characteristically such a company is well established, does not attempt to 'steal' your ideas or customers and, most importantly, does not perceive you as a threat, so there is a state of peaceful co-existence. You may be happy with this situation and in fact if the competitor is much more powerful than yourself you might even be glad of it. However this cosy situation may not go on forever so their activities must be monitored to detect any change in the status quo.

Potentially dangerous signs are when such a competitor: has a change of senior management, or moves into larger premises, or takes over another business, or raises money on the Stock Exchange (where such action is at least public) or starts recruiting more sales staff or launches a new product/service similar to your own. Any of these actions might indicate an impending change in the status quo with the "benign" competitor becoming more "hostile". For other tips see the earlier Chapter **Watching The Competition**.

HOSTILE COMPETITORS

In contrast to a "benign" competitor, a "hostile" one poses a threat (or it may be multiple threats!) to your business as they are actively pursuing your customers to gain market share at your expense. The degree of hostility can range from what outsiders might class as "healthy competition" (it never feels quite so healthy when it involves you yourself) to positively "pathological". In the latter category your competitor attempts to make you either cease trading or at least move out of that market sector entirely and they are prepared to go to considerable lengths, and expense, to accomplish that objective. Elaborate plans will be devised by such competitors whose sole objective is to disable you and some of their tactics may be unethical and possibly even illegal. Typical tactics include: poaching your key staff; spreading "disinformation" about your business to mutual customers; directing media attention to any weakness or problems you may have; engaging you in a price war; stealing your customers; taking legal action against you or interfering with your sources of supply or your distribution channels.

When confronted by any hostile competitor, your first action must be to learn as much as possible about them as described in the Chapter **Watching The Competition**. Next you have to deal with the threat(s) they pose. Let us consider the various threats mentioned above and how they may be countered.

Poaching Staff If you have key staff who are critical to your smooth operation, losing them could present two main threats. First, they may take sensitive inside knowledge of your operation to your competitor and second, they may have skills which are difficult to replace quickly. Taking these two aspects separately, you should be careful how much commercial information any one member of staff has access to. A little thought will indicate "Top Secret" subjects which should either never be discussed with employed staff (and any relevant files should be locked away) or parts of those subjects should be revealed only on a clear "need to know" basis.

"I hear that new firm is offering some catchy incentives...."

The second aspect usually occurs in a small business where one employee becomes the best at doing a particular skilled activity and soon gains considerable expertise which if lost would present a problem for the business. The solution is to ensure every key operator has a deputy whom you ensure has at least a basic working knowledge and could therefore fill the breach if the "No 1" departs suddenly (or simply takes ill or is injured).

In a more positive vein, staff poaching can also be combated by generating a team spirit, looking after staff and rewarding them (initially verbally, then financially and later by increased responsibility and promotion) so their incentive to move will be much reduced. A further means of reducing key staff turnover is a **Contract of Employment** which may discourage them from leaving before the end of the Contract period.

Disinformation/Media Essentially this is a propaganda campaign which can be very effective so needs to be countered. Frequently the information that is spread about you will be misleading and done verbally without witnesses so there is unlikely to be recourse through libel or slander litigation. As always, some mud inevitably sticks.

Propaganda can be fought by a counter-propaganda campaign which need not simply be defensive trying to set the record straight but might also attack the competition to put them on the defensive (though first take appropriate legal advice on this). But perhaps the best way of beating any propaganda is to win the hearts and minds of your customers — to woo them, keep them informed, well-looked after and therefore loyal.

Price War Like any war this is costly for all sides and if it develops into a war of attrition it can spell the end for the smaller business with its weaker resources, or might even lead to the demise of both businesses. In general, price wars are a bad thing to be avoided at all costs but if a competitor's actions unavoidably draws you into such a conflict it is important to have a feel for the situation and to take what action you can.

The biggest threat is when your competitor is merely a branch of a larger company. In that case they can drop their prices locally against you and keep them low almost indefinitely (until you go bust) as the profits from their other branches can finance this.

An easier situation from your viewpoint is when the competitor is a single operation and so the drop in prices will hurt them as much as you.

So how should you respond if a competitor drops its price? The first point is that it is not always necessary to drop prices in order to compete! The factors which are relevant are: the price sensitivity of your commodity (eg food items are price sensitive as people know the prices and one pint of milk appears to the buyer much like any other pint of milk); how often a customer uses you or your competitor (ie is the trade "passing" and always changing or the same group returning); convenience (this could be very relevant); special features (ie if you have features which your competitor does not, this may save you having to fully drop your prices).

Stealing Customers Although a competitor who is spreading propaganda and dropping its prices is obviously trying to steal your customers, more direct action may be used. For instance, if your business depends on a relatively small number of customers (as is often the case in a business-to-business situation) the competitor may visit each of your main customers and offer various inducements to encourage them to use the competitor rather than your business. You need to face up to such direct action by ensuring you make contact yourself with such buyers.

Legal Action There would have to be some pretext, however small, for a competitor even to contemplate some form of legal proceedings. However, it is not unknown for large companies to start proceedings the outcome of which any Court would be unlikely to find in their favour, but the threat often succeeds in obtaining an out-of-Court settlement to their advantage. Usually alleged breach of trading name, brand or logo or alleged copying of a product are the type of pretext the other company's solicitors look for. Should any form of legal proceedings be started against you, get the best and most competent legal advice straight away and it may also be prudent to set aside a "fighting fund" just in case.

Interference Another popular tactic used by hostile competitors is to interfere with your sources of supply or distribution. It is only normally relevant if there is a limited number of such suppliers and if the competitor purchases considerably larger quantities than you do. This can be a serious problem if it occurs and will require you to take action. Visiting your suppliers and making personal contact can help

Coping With Competitors

but often the only choice is to quickly try to locate alternative suppliers even if they are abroad. Another, more subtle, approach is to find an ally who the supplier values (or fears) and who is prepared to have a word in their ear on your behalf. Perhaps it may be one of their suppliers! Distribution is usually more difficult for anyone to interfere with but it is still worth taking a moment to consider how you might be vulnerable and to then do something about it before your competitor does!

The Direct Copy Competitor

A particularly irritating form of competition is the "me-too" copy. Companies that appear to be doing well and have an easy market entry threshold are particularly vulnerable to this type of competition (see also the item on market entry in the Chapter earlier in this book, **Assessing A New Project**). It is sometimes quite surprising just how close a copy such a competitor is and one wonders at their obvious lack of imagination and ethics. It may be some consolation to the original business that the success rate of "me-too" copies is low. This is possibly due to them having less market knowledge and the obvious disadvantage of being the second (or third or whatever) in the field.

However, in the short term such a competitor is a threat and may take some of your market share.

When faced with a new "me-too" competitor you must initially assume it is a hostile competitor and you need to take the appropriate actions outlined above.

Indirect Competition

There is another type of competitor and that is the "indirect" competitor as mentioned at the start of this Chapter. You may focus too much attention on direct competitors who are in your own trade sector and in so doing you might miss the significance of an outside indirect threat.

The subject of indirect competition is also relevant in terms of how a business promotes itself. You should ask yourself the question "What business am I in?" as the answer is not necessarily obvious. For instance, a manufacturer of high quality preserves which are packaged in attractive jars might carry out an analysis of sales to indicate the types of outlets that are buying their product. The result might be that 80% are sold to gift shops, rather than food outlets. This reveals that the business is in the gift trade, rather than the food industry, when it comes to thinking of marketing and sales. Direct competitors may be others making similar preserves but indirect competitors will be all those other firms that make small desirable gifts at the same price point and aimed at similar buyers.

Avoiding Confrontation

As a small business, you cannot afford more competition than necessary and certainly you are unlikely to survive a confrontation with a major corporation. So how can you reduce the chances of such a conflict?

The first point to realise is that all businesses have what they perceive as their own "territory". This may not be simply a geographical delineation but can extend to product ranges, areas of service and so on. If you therefore encroach on a major company's territory, the company is unlikely to ignore this for long. You should also think carefully (and take legal advice) before referring to competitors in any advertising or sales literature you produce.

It is probably better to avoid direct confrontation and seek niches of the market which the larger competitor is ignoring, at least until you are strong enough to make more direct moves.

Also, keep a low profile, ie do not invite a counter-attack from large companies. They will probably ignore you if they think that your operation is insignificant.

Who Wins?

A final, slightly sobering thought on the subject of competition. Where there is a competitive struggle, it is not necessarily the best or cheapest product or service that is the ultimate winner. How a business is marketed, promoted and sold can count for more than the product or service itself in the long run ∎

Confronting No Growth or Rapid Growth

No growth or rapid growth are two very contrasting types of special situation which merit attention. Many businesses would not necessarily regard themselves as having a problem if they were either having no growth or enjoying rapid growth, but this may not be the case.

NO GROWTH

This describes a business where the level of sales is such that all overheads are met and the Proprietors or Directors take out some remuneration, but the business is static and shows no sign of growth or even of consolidation. Americans, perhaps rather cruelly, call this type of business "the living dead". Those businesses that have cashflow problems may envy such a situation but really it is not very healthy for by being static a business can be quite vulnerable for two reasons. First its lack of growth suggests it is not probing new markets or trying out new products or services and in a changing market place it could find itself unexpectedly obsolete. Second, it may be producing insufficient reserves for future contingencies.

It is not that the pursuit of growth in itself need be an objective, rather that the lack of growth may be a symptom of underlying problems such as a declining market or being tied to just a handful of large customers.

The normal route out of this situation is to continue with the present business relatively unchanged (as it is, after all, viable) but to make time, staff and cash increasingly available for diversification.

The major stumbling block which prevents a business in this predicament from taking any action is usually a degree of complacency or resistance with the management. To overcome any in-built inertia in the business, fresh management talent could be brought in even if only for a short period. For instance, a consultant or a summer vacation student could look at different options. See also the notes on brainstorming and diversifying in the Chapter **Solving A Cashflow Problem.**

CONTROLLED GROWTH

A problem that faces every small business as it starts to expand is just how should it grow? Initially extra staff might be taken on to cope with the increasing workload but that brings its own problems as precious management time is spent recruiting, training and supervising the new staff. But what other alternatives could be considered?

1. Using Other People   You might sub-contract out part of your work to another company. Or rather than taking on new staff you might be able to use "out-workers" or "cottage workers" or self-employed Agents. But beware – employment law now regards some of these "self-employed" people as being, in fact, employees. So do first take legal advice if considering this option.

2. Bringing In New Partners/ Directors   Since management time and ability will be in short supply (and capital too probably) as the business grows, it might be worth considering inviting someone you know and trust (in a business sense) to be a Partner or Director. But interview them thoroughly, ensure their business ethics are sound and their personal finances are in good shape.

3. Franchising   Business Format Franchising is an interesting option for many service businesses to consider if they have a local customer base and the business format can be replicated in other towns across the country. It is an increasingly popular method for rapid growth but to do professionally it takes a great deal of time and effort to set up a franchise.

Many franchise operators are members of the British Franchise Association, Thames View, Newtown Road, Henley-on-Thames, Oxon RG9 1HG. Tel: (0491) 578049. See also the box on Franchising over the page.

"I don't know what I've done – but it must be right!"

Confronting No Growth or Rapid Growth

4. Expanding by Acquisition Even a small company can expand greatly, and quickly, by buying over another business to give it increased market share, more control of its outlets, more buying power or perhaps access to more production capacity.

5. Licensing Rather than handling new markets yourself, you might license existing companies to do that for you.

At this stage, you should also get good tax advice to ensure the proposed structure of the business is such that future tax liabilities are minimised.

RAPID GROWTH

In many ways this is the dream of most entrepreneurs but it is not without its own problems which are worth considering and planning for.

As turnover rises steeply, normally one of the first problems is that your cash requirements increase in tandem due to the need for more stock and/or having more customers on credit. This cash is normally found by increasing the overdraft — a debt which has to be financed and eventually repaid, so needs watching. In addition the business may need more staff and possibly equipment, vehicles and new premises. Staff require selection, training and supervising, all of which will create their own problems for the small business. Employing staff is covered in detail in a companion book, titled *The (Greatest) Little Business Book.*

An increase in sales may not be sustained in the longer term and if sales drop you may find you have taken on too many new commitments. This drop in sales might occur because your success has attracted "me-too" style competitors who are now taking some of your market share.

After a period of rapid growth, the real Achilles Heel is likely to be inadequate management procedures. These procedures might have been adequate at one time but have probably not been adapted to meet the new demands for controlling cash, staff, stock, credit and so on. The consolation is that this is one of the easiest aspects to put right in a business, if necessary by bringing in management consultancy assistance ■

FRANCHISING

What Is Franchising? This is when an established successful business is prepared to sell someone a licence (called a "franchise") to operate a business using its name, its image, its business knowledge, its back-up — in fact the whole proven business format. The advantage to the purchaser (called the "franchisee") is that they are taking on a proven business format and will be given training and back-up which should increase the chances of their success. In addition to an initial fee, the franchisee pays a royalty to the "franchisor" but in return will expect on-going support, long term market research to ensure the business keeps up to date, advertising support, trouble-shooting and, very importantly, an exclusive territory.

When the franchisee starts trading, there is an Operations Manual which lays down exactly how the business is to be run. In good franchise operations the franchisor works closely with their franchisees to ensure the business makes profits and conforms to the franchise agreement. This is in the franchisor's interest as the franchisee pays a royalty, calculated as a fixed weekly or monthly amount or as a percentage (typically 2%-20%) of sales.

The rights and obligations of both parties are described in a contract which is a very detailed document and forms the basis of the close association.

Why Franchise? Companies often franchise because they can expand more quickly than by opening conventional branches and the finance to open these outlets comes mainly from the franchisees. The Head Office management structure is also slimmer in a franchise operation and the franchisees are usually more motivated (as it is their own business).

Can You Franchise? Typically, potential franchisors are retail or service businesses which are profitable, can operate regionally or nationally through similar outlets and, most importantly, have some unique aspect such as an identifiable image, process etc. Manufacturers have more difficulty in franchising unless they set up tied outlets for their products or have a product suitable for local manufacture, eg window blinds or fitted kitchens.

Setting Up A Franchise Done properly this is both time consuming and expensive. The preparation of the contract and Operations Manual can take man-years of work and 5-figure sums as they must be done thoroughly. The proper marketing of the franchise and the careful selection of franchisees takes further time and expense. Expert advice is essential.

INDEX

Great Books For Small Business . . .

The Greatest Little Business Book
The Essential Guide to Starting a Small Business

A comprehensive, yet readable, reference book. A best-seller and highly recommended by small business advisers. Many worked examples, eg Cashflow Forecast, Business Plan and a Partnership Agreement. Also: legalities, raising finance, finding premises, employing staff, tax & VAT. Updated annually. 120 pages with many illustrations. by **Peter Hingston** **£7.50**

The Greatest Sales & Marketing Book
The Practical Action Guide for a Small Business

Full of ideas to increase your sales. How to advertise successfully. Many worked examples, eg Pricing, a Press Release and Leaflet. Tips to survive a Recession. Hints to avoid losing sales. Advice to keep down overheads. Market Research – how to do it and how it helps. The book has had many excellent reviews, for example, *The Times, Money Week* and *British Business* magazine. Updated regularly. 120 pages and highly illustrated. by **Peter Hingston** **£7.50**

The Greatest Guide to Home-based Business
101 Great Business Ideas plus How to Work from Home

Working from home is the growth area of new businesses in the 1990s. This book is co-authored by Eric Smith, Australia's leading author on small business subjects. In addition to advice on starting a business in Britain, it covers the particular problems of working from home. The book also features 101 great business ideas to inspire the reader.
120 pages and illustrated. by **Peter Hingston & Eric Smith** **£7.95**

The Best Accounts Books
For non-VAT (and VAT) registered Small Businesses

These accounts books were launched in late 1991 and are fast becoming class leaders. Written in layman's language, with a simple and attractive format and full instructions. Suitable for most businesses (sole traders, partnerships or limited companies). Choose between the YELLOW BOOK (for a *cash* business) or the BLUE BOOK (for a *credit* business). A4 size, hardcover. **£7.99**

The BLUE BOOK is also available in a VAT version with extra columns for VAT, a complete VAT Section and help to complete your VAT Returns. **£9.99**